GILBERT HARDING

A

Gilbert Harding leaving University College Hospital, followed by the author.

GILBERT HARDING

BY HIS PRIVATE SECRETARY
ROGER STOREY

LONDON
BARRIE AND ROCKLIFF

Printed in Great Britain by
The Anchor Press,
Tiptree, Essex.

CONTENTS

ILLUSTRATIONS

PREFACE

I WOULD like to preface this book with a disclaimer. I have neither
the knowledge nor the experience to attempt a biography, still less
a psychological study of Gilbert Harding. All I wish to do is to
present a picture of the man I worked for in as detached a manner
as may be possible for someone who has been so closely involved with
his daily life.

It was he who first put the idea into my mind. Three or four
years before his death he first referred to 'the book you will write
about me', and I accepted it as a joke. But, reading the continual
comments in the press, listening to adulation and criticism from all
kinds of people who knew only the public face of my employer,
finally one day I decided that I would try to write about the reality.

There were several reason for my decision. Firstly, whenever
anyone discovered what my job was they began to ask, 'What is
he really like? . . . Is it true that he is just acting when he loses
his temper on *What's My Line?* . . . Can he really cook? . . .'

Secondly, I felt that because the name of Gilbert Harding will
be long loved and remembered in the hearts of thousands of people,
some such record should be written. Since he had no close relations,
I felt I was the only one who knew him well enough to do so.

Thirdly, I have written it for myself, while it is still fresh in my
mind, for I know that had I not set it all down, a lot of it would
have faded from my memory in a year or two. And I do not want
to lose those eight years when I was Gilbert Harding's secretary.
If, when I first took on the job, I had known all that I later learned
about my employer, I should never have dared to do so. I am glad
I did not know. I am quite certain that for the rest of my life
I shall look upon those years as the richest and most exciting I
have ever experienced.

'MR. HARDING NEEDS A SECRETARY'

'How would you like to be Gilbert Harding's secretary?' Frame asked as we met by appointment on the stairs.

'Not much,' I said. 'Why?'

Frame was Miss Frame-Smith, a colleague in Adprint, the London publishing firm where I worked.

'Gilbert had dinner with us last night,' she explained. 'He said he needed someone to look after him. And I suggested you. Just *think* about it now and we'll talk properly another time. But it won't do any harm to consider it.'

It certainly needed a lot of consideration. It was April 1952 and I was twenty-seven. I was a secretary from necessity, not persuasion. Originally I had been an actor – and less successful than most. As with many actors and actresses, when work was scarce and money scarcer, I had worked for secretarial agencies as a temporary typist.

Slowly, and very reluctantly, I had come to the conclusion that I had very little future as an actor. But I was a pretty competent typist. The trouble was that I didn't like office work – not until I spent a few days as holiday relief with Adprint. There the atmosphere was so friendly and informal, so different from any other office I had worked in, that I actually enjoyed the work. I decided to ask if they could find me a permanent job. They promised to remember me when there was a vacancy, and about six weeks later, in November, I was offered a permanent job, to start the following January, and accepted at once.

Almost immediately, of course, other offers came. There was a small part in a documentary film, and then a two weeks' 'guest' engagement at the Darlington Repertory Theatre. Darlington is only thirty miles from my north Yorkshire home, so I went to stay with my parents until after my last appearance on the stage.

The last Saturday of the fortnight was in many senses a very special occasion. My parents, who had never seen me act, were there. The play was *Parnell*, the name-part was played by Leslie Randall, Kitty O'Shea by Joan Reynolds (now the famous television 'Joan and Leslie'), and I was one of Parnell's elderly and loyal supporters. The final appearance of Roger Storey, actor, was crowned by an enthusiastic round of applause when I made my first exit.

Thirty-six hours later I started my new job of typing labels for the export edition of a business magazine published by Adprint. It was difficult at first to settle down to the strangeness of regular hours and the new horror of travelling in London during the rush periods. It didn't make it any easier to remember that I had been offered the chance of staying on at Darlington and, for the first time in months, my telephone rang regularly with offers of stage and film work.

But I liked my new colleagues. I liked the regular weekly pay packet. And when, a few weeks later, Darlington Repertory Theatre closed down for good I knew that I had been right to make up my mind to steady office work.

When Frame talked to me on the stairs I had then gradually been promoted from label-typing to the grand title of 'assistant secretary' to the kindly managing director, Mr. Wolfgang Foges.

It was the next day before Frame and I could meet outside the office for an explanation of her fantastic suggestion. Over a cup of coffee she explained that Mr. Harding, then in the first flush of his fame on *What's My Line?* had been telling her about his mounting correspondence, engagements and business affairs, and lamenting that he had no full-time help. He only had a former secretary, now married, who came in two or three hours a day once or twice a week. That wasn't nearly enough. Surely, he had said, Frame must know of someone who might take a permanent job as his secretary.

I was flattered that she should have suggested me, but wary. I knew very little about Gilbert Harding. And I didn't particularly like the little I knew. I didn't have (and still haven't) a television set, but I had seen him once or twice on *What's My Line?* and, of course, had read the newspaper accounts of his fiery outbursts on that programme and elsewhere. Only a few weeks before he had once again hit the headlines. One of the challengers of *What's My Line?* had been a professional ghost hunter, so Gilbert had asked him if he really believed in ghosts. When the challenger said that naturally he did, Gilbert barked out, 'Then you must be barmy!' The fact that he apologized in the programme the following week had only added to the publicity.

On another occasion he had told a challenger that he was tired of looking at his face, and to another – a *restaurateur* – that he would find out the name of his restaurant and be certain to avoid it. Both these incidents had been splashed by the press, but the really sensational treatment had been given to the programme when on his own admission Harding had taken part in the game when he was 'a little bit tiddly'.

It seemed that everyone who had a television set tuned in to *What's My Line?* every week, eagerly hoping that Gilbert would provide some scandalous gossip. Later I was to find that Gilbert referred to such unfortunate events as 'disfiguring incidents'.

Recently, too, his face had appeared on the hoardings on a new *People* poster: there was one opposite the railway station at Penge, where I lived. It was a scraper-board drawing, about twenty times larger than life, showing him in his most ferocious, glowering mood. Seeing it every morning as I started for the office almost made me flinch.

But I believed, as so many people apparently still do, that his outbursts of temper, his dogmatic statements and his brick-dropping owed a great deal to his keen awareness of their publicity-value. Just previously I had been intensely irritated by an ill-informed, illogical and bigoted anti-ballet article he had written for *Illustrated*. I felt he was just joining in the popular pastime of debunking other people's tastes.

On the other hand, Frame, who had known him when she was in the B B C monitoring service during the war, had often told me that Gilbert was one of the kindest, most hospitable, and most amusing men she had ever known. She admitted that he probably drank too much and too often, and that he had a fiery temper. But, she assured me, his outbursts were usually brief and quickly forgotten. He always regretted them.

I had been deeply impressed, too, by a recent broadcast on Boxing Day in which Gilbert Harding had said so many things that needed saying: about the awful, shoddy commercialism of Christmas, with its decorated shops full of tawdry rubbish, the

greetings cards that had nothing at all to do with the birth of
Christ, and the dreadful tit-for-tat present-giving. And he had read,
very movingly, a tribute to the Puritans from the great essayist
Macaulay.

To me – as to very many people who knew him only as a member of panel games – it was an introduction to an unknown Harding.
The man who made that Boxing Day broadcast was sentimental and
sincere. But not uncomplicated: for who else would have chosen
for such an occasion a reading from an Osbert Sitwell essay on cigar-
box labels?

So I agreed with Frame that, even though I might not want to
take the job, it would be an interesting experience to meet him.

I am in most circumstances a rather shy and diffident man, so
it took a great deal of courage the next morning to lift the telephone and dial the number Frame had given me. But Mr. Harding's
immediate warmth and friendliness at the other end of the line
reassured me, and when he arranged that I should have lunch with
him early the following week in his flat at Cadogan Place I began to
look forward to it.

Now my conviction that I wouldn't like to work for him began
to waver. During the weekend that followed I spent a lot of time
wondering and worrying about it. Still, Frame had warned me
that Gilbert was erratic, and that frequently his enthusiasms petered
out as swiftly as they had been fired. So I realized that the final
decision might well be out of my hands. Or perhaps, when we met,
he would consider me quite unsuitable for the job: then there
would be no decision to make.

There was another problem, too. My position at Adprint was
reasonably assured. If I left to become the secretary of a 'star of
radio and television', could I be sure that he would remain so for
much longer. Harding's rise to notoriety had been loud and swift.
Could his popularity last? If it didn't, he certainly wouldn't need
a secretary!

The morning of the day on which I was to have this important
lunch was one of the most hectic I had spent at Adprint. Mr. Foges
was leaving that evening for a business trip to the United States
and there were a hundred and one essential, last-minute matters
to be settled. But at one o'clock I managed to find a taxi and,
worrying myself into a sweat of nervousness, urged it to 18 Cadogan
Place.

I arrived at ten past one, expecting to find my host in a fury. But he wasn't.

'You said you would be here *about* one o'clock,' he said. 'It's only ten minutes past now.'

In any case, there was no sign of lunch, and the chaos I had left behind me at Adprint seemed peaceful compared to this flat. A television producer and his two assistants were trying to discuss a programme with Mr. Harding, and though they were in a hurry to leave – or so they said – the discussions showed no signs of finishing. And they were punctuated every few minutes by the telephone bell. One of the calls was from someone – I think it was Maurice Winnick – who wanted to see Gilbert urgently. Could he come round, just for ten minutes, at once? He did, and stayed for half an hour.

He arrived just as the two assistants had left, and Gilbert suggested I might sit down with a drink until they had had their talk. He led me into the kitchen. He had already told me we were to have lunch in there and hoped I didn't mind the informality. In fact, I was rather touched that such a famous man could still live so simply and unostentatiously.

Before he left me there, he introduced me to Mrs. Clarke. She was the wife of the caretaker, and she took a particular pride in looking after the television star. She told me that she was over sixty, but still got up before four o'clock every morning to supervise the cleaners in a big office in the City. And she announced that, we were to have fried fish and *sauté* potatoes, cooked by her, for lunch.

'Mr. Harding always tells me nobody fries fish as well as I do. Of course, I should, mind you. I fried fish in Barker's restaurant for twenty years.'

Later I was to learn the curious mathematics of Mrs. Clarke's working life, for though she seemed to have had a number of different jobs each one of them had been for twenty years. She had been a chambermaid at several West End hotels, and her stories of the 'goings on' at these places were usually unrepeatable.

Because she was opposed to change of any kind, Mrs. Clarke was a little suspicious of me at first, but we became very good friends, and for the next twelve months I was to find her the proverbial tower of strength. Her kindness, generosity and humour – and her energy – were amazing, and her friendship helped me through many difficult times.

At just about the time I should have been on my way back to

the office, lunch was ready and Gilbert was free to eat. Though I had so far exchanged few words with him, his pleasant and friendly manner was beginning to win me over. In spite of the chaos, the incessant ringing of the telephone and other interruptions, he remained good-humoured and unruffled. I began to think my mental picture of him had been wildly wrong. But I was a bit put out to find that the television producer was to stay to lunch. I was afraid that this would make any kind of discussion of my possible job rather difficult and, for me anyway, somewhat embarrassing. I needn't have worried, for the business that had brought me to Cadogan Place was the one subject we never really got around to.

Nevertheless, as I was to discover, had Gilbert wanted to discuss my prospects of getting the job he would not have taken the visitor into account. It was one of the charming things about him that he never had any business secrets and was always quite happy – though often I wasn't – to discuss the most private financial matters in front of anyone who happened to be there.

I was to discover, too, that some of my new conceptions of him were as false as the old. That morning was almost the last occasion on which I was to see him remain calm and good-humoured in the midst of confusion. Those simple, unaffected kitchen lunches were on their way out also. Gradually meals at Cadogan Place, and subsequently at his flat in Weymouth Street and his house in Brighton, became more elaborate.

Soon it became obvious that Gilbert had already made up his mind that I would be suitable for the job, and by now all doubts about it had left me. I wanted the job very much indeed. We briefly mentioned money and hours. At the time I was getting nine pounds a week. He said he would pay me nine pounds ten, to be increased to ten pounds after three months. Four years later, by stages, this figure had been doubled. When, later, he turned himself into a limited company, which became my employer, I got a generous bonus every year on top of my regular salary.

Then we turned to hours. Mr. Harding suggested I should start at ten o'clock. Flushed with enthusiasm, I said that I was used to being on the job by nine-fifteen each morning and, if it would be any help, I would do the same for him. 'Well, now, wouldn't that be nice?' he beamed. 'After all, you'll very rarely have to stay any later than five in the afternoon.'

That beam was full of goodwill, and I am certain he believed the

Gilbert Harding investigates for *The People*. With Mr. W. E. Hurst and his son Raymond, at Middleyard Stroud.

With David Niven and Dora Bryan.

(*Associated British Picture Corporation photograph*)

At the microphone during *Purely For Pleasure*. The producer, John Lade (with cigarette) is behind in the control room.

In hospital, but still keeping up with the programmes.

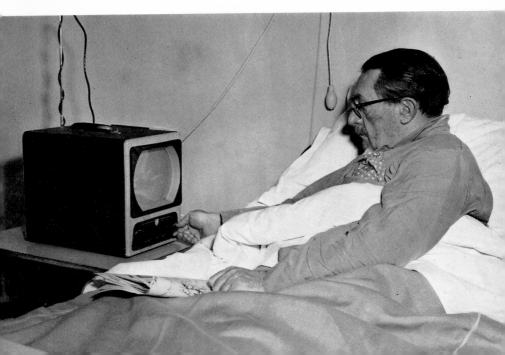

words as he said them. In practice I never once heard that 'down tools' at five o'clock throughout the years that I was his secretary. I never left earlier than six and very often it was seven or eight o'clock: sometimes very much later than that.

Of course, he wanted me to start working for him right away. Whatever Mr. Harding wanted, he wanted it there and then. But I had to give a month's notice to Adprint and, though I hoped they would be understanding and let me leave sooner, I might have to stay the full four weeks.

I arrived back at the office over an hour late and a little intoxicated with wine and brandy, but much more with my host's larger-than-life exuberance and personality. I walked into an atmosphere of cold disapproval that I should have stayed out so long on such a busy day. It was not easy to explain to Joyce Howell, Mr. Foges's secretary, just what had kept me, but I felt I ought to tell the managing director before he left for America because I would be gone before his return.

Joyce was her usual pleasant, kindly self, and I sobered up when she said they would miss me. Still, she agreed that I must tell Mr. Foges, but how? Directors and executives were in and out of his office on last-minute errands, and he himself kept diving into other offices with final instructions. It wasn't made any easier when he popped his head into my office to ask what size collar I wore – he intended to buy me a nylon shirt in New York. (It was a typical Foges action that the shirt was sent to me at Cadogan Place a few weeks later!) Then Joyce was called into his room for dictation. She was out again in a few moments with the message that Mr. Foges wanted to see me at once. She had told him.

He was as understanding as I had expected. He even said that Gilbert Harding was a very lucky man and that he himself was most disappointed that I was leaving Adprint. The last of my exuberance faded. I was so moved that I was very tempted to say that it was all a mistake and of course I wouldn't dream of leaving. But I didn't.

Two days later Frame asked me to ring Gilbert – urgently. He said he wanted to see me again as something rather important had occurred to him, so I arranged to go to Cadogan Place the following Saturday evening. I was quite sure he must have changed his mind about giving me the job. I felt sick with disappointment and the certainty of a humiliating anti-climax.

When I arrived at the flat I was nervous and tense, and G.H.

B

looked quite stern and serious. He gave me a seat and a drink. 'I've been thinking about this job,' he began, and my mouth went dry. 'I realize that you have a good job now, with a good firm, and that you are happy in it. And I am quite sure that you could be just as happy working for me. But how long will it last?'

I kept quiet. I was just beginning to think I knew what was in his mind.

'I'm a television notoriety now. But in two years – in one year, even – where will I be? And is that a good, steady prospect for a young man like you? I just want to make sure that you know exactly what you are doing in agreeing to work for me.'

I took a good pull at my drink, allowed myself to breathe again, and told him happily that I was fully aware of the situation, that I didn't mind at all, and was more than willing to take the risk of his fading into obscurity.

So that was settled. And on Monday, 18th May, 1953, I reported at Cadogan Place for my first day's work as 'secretary to Mr. Gilbert Harding'.

CHAPTER TWO

NEW MASTER, NEW MAN

On the first day of my job I arrived at the corner of Cadogan Place and Pont Street at exactly ten minutes past nine.

I have always hated to be unpunctual, and that morning I was determined to show my new employer that my late arrival for the first meeting a few weeks earlier was not typical of me. I waited on the corner until it was nine-fourteen a.m. and at exactly nine-fifteen I rang his front-door bell. After a few seconds there was a loud *click*, as though the lock had slipped into place, but no one came to the door. A minute later – though it seemed more like five – I rang again. Again there was a click, but nothing more. Suddenly, through the glass panel of the front door, I saw Gilbert, in pyjamas and dressing-gown, coming towards me.

'My dear boy,' he exclaimed, as he pulled the door open, 'when you hear that click you are meant to push the door and walk in. When the door bell rings, I press a switch in the flat and in you come.' My face must have shown what a fool I felt. Harding beamed. 'But how were you to know?'

He led me into the kitchen, where he was finishing his breakfast. 'Get yourself a cup and have some coffee, too, while I tell you what's going on today,' he suggested. 'What's going on?' was one of Gilbert's favourite phrases. As soon as he got home from some outside engagement or whenever he telephoned to the flat, his first question was usually, 'What's going on?' It was rarely easy to summarize, in the few words he seemed to expect, all that had been happening during the day, but eventually I realized that the answer, 'Oh, nothing very much', usually satisfied him.

On that first morning the table where we sat was littered with letters and opened envelopes which had come in the early post. 'All rubbish,' Gilbert exclaimed, 'but we'll have to try and answer them before I go out. If you can find a notebook and pencils among that mess in the dining-room we might as well start.'

I found them and came back to the kitchen, silently praying that he would not dictate too quickly – because I couldn't write shorthand! He knew it, of course. I had told him myself at my first interview. Indeed, I had half-hoped, in the strange uncertainty of my wishes then, that such a drawback would at once rule me out. Even after I had been engaged I had asked Frame to make my ignorance quite clear to him, because I had felt that perhaps he hadn't realized how important it might be. At one time I had tried to learn shorthand at evening classes, but however hard I studied – both at school and at home – I had found it so dreadfully difficult that I finally abandoned the attempt. Then, when I started in my first real job with Adprint, I discovered that I could take dictation in my own abbreviated kind of handwriting almost as quickly – and certainly just as accurately – as many shorthand-writers could.

All this I had explained to Gilbert when I first met him. He seemed to think it supremely unimportant. 'I always dictate very slowly,' he said. 'In any case, if you're any good at all, after a week or two you will be able to answer most of the letters yourself without dictation. Then all I shall have to do is to sign them.'

Of course, he always dictated articles and scripts and letters to personal friends, but eventually I found that I was able to cope with about half of each day's post without referring to Gilbert at all. It was true that when he did dictate – even after he had realized that I could quite comfortably keep up with him – he rarely increased the speed. Nor did he mind if, when I could not read what I had written, I had to ask him to repeat what he had said.

Nevertheless, he always took mischievous pleasure in teasing me about my lack of shorthand – it was part of the gleeful malice of his nature. On the first occasion that I met Leslie Jackson, who was then the producer of *What's My Line?* Gilbert suggested that I should challenge the panel as the only private secretary who couldn't write a stroke of shorthand.

I had certainly never written a fan letter in my life. Until that first morning at Cadogan Place I hadn't even seen one. I hadn't supposed that, outside the organized fan clubs, many people had the time or inclination to write them. But although there was no Gilbert Harding Fan Club, each day brought dozens of letters, mostly expressions of affection and appreciation, from readers, listeners and viewers. That mail on the kitchen table, my first day at work, was mainly from admirers and from those who asked him to open garden parties, fêtes or bazaars, or to attend some public function to draw the crowds.

We had managed to deal with the mail by the time Gilbert had to get dressed for his first appointment, a publicity luncheon given by a wine-importing firm . . . 'I expect I shall be back rather late,' he said.

I was left with a pile of letters, a book half-full of dictated replies – and very little idea of where to find paper, envelopes, and all the other things I was likely to need. The previous week I had arranged to come to Cadogan Place one lunch-time so that the woman whose job I was taking over could show me the ropes. I hadn't expected to find Gilbert there that day, but he was; and by the time he had offered me a drink and talked to me I had only about ten minutes left to talk to my predecessor. So for my first few weeks I had to find my own way round and learn by trial and error. Gilbert himself knew very little about the methods of filing and book-keeping, so he was not much help – particularly as he didn't seem to care either.

I had always worked before in the company of plenty of other people. It was a strange feeling to be left entirely on my own to get on with the job. Particularly in that flat. I realized for the first time how gloomy it was.

The big windows of the sitting-room faced on to the gardens of Cadogan Place, and it was the one light and cheerful room in the whole flat. From the sitting-room a long, many-angled corridor led past the spare room to the bathroom, the kitchen, Gilbert's bedroom, and the dining-room – my 'office'. The office was light enough, but the windows were set so high in the wall that it wasn't possible to see out of them. The furniture was of heavy, sombre oak and the carpet and curtains were brown. The general effect was of a large, light cell. Gilbert's bedroom was a little more pleasant only because he had added a few of his own possessions to the sturdy furniture provided by the landlord.

I remember how incensed Mrs. Clarke was when Nancy Spain once wrote that Gilbert Harding had invited her round to 'his hideous flat in Cadogan Square'. It wasn't only the word 'hideous' that had upset Mrs. Clarke – she found it equally difficult to forgive Miss Spain for not knowing her 'Place' from her 'Square'!

It was a great shock to me when, only a few days after my job started, there arrived the bill for a quarter's rent for the flat – at fourteen guineas a week. I was horrified that anyone should calmly pay so much money for so much ugliness.

Because of the way the dining-room furniture was arranged, I found that I had to sit typing with my back to the door. And because of the fact that the room was at the end of the long corridor it was quite possible for someone with a key to the front door to appear silently beside me as I worked. After a few days of being constantly surprised by either Gilbert or Mrs. Clarke I rearranged the tables and chairs so that I could face the door while I typed.

This first morning, though, as I was just settling down, having searched for paper, carbons, envelopes and rubber, Mrs. Clarke appeared at my side. She wondered if I would be going out for lunch or if I would like her to give me 'something light'. I thought that by not going out I could save time and perhaps finish typing all the morning's letters by the time my boss got back. The 'something light' turned out to be a lavish helping of cold tongue and salad, followed by a baked sponge pudding and cheese, all brought up from her basement flat.

So, unwittingly, I set the pattern of the future. Throughout my job as Gilbert Harding's secretary I lunched, almost without exception, in his home. That hour's break from bustle and tension which most people get in a commercial job was never mine. If I was alone, I had what was going – even if it was a sandwich I made for myself from whatever was in the refrigerator or the larder. If Mr. Harding was there we lunched together – sometimes very well, at a restaurant or at his club, sometimes at home with a snack. I even learned, when he had important visitors, to help in the preparation and serving of some of his favourite, enticing recipes. Luckily I was already interested in cooking before I took the job.

I scarcely gave myself time, that day, to enjoy the lunch Mrs. Clarke provided. I rushed back to my typewriter to get on with the work and, by the time Gilbert returned, at about five o'clock, the letters were all finished.

But I quickly realized that they wouldn't be signed that day. The wine-importers had obviously been generous with their goods. He was very drunk. 'This is what Frame told me about,' I thought, as my stomach seemed to tie itself into a shrinking knot. He was gay, outrageous, furious, friendly, grumbling, roaring with laughter – all in turn. And no turn lasted for more than a few minutes.

Fortunately for me he had brought home with him a friend whom he had seen in the street and hailed from his taxi. This was a man who had been a close friend of Gilbert's since his early days with the B B C, and it was soon obvious that he had many times coped with similar situations in the past.

That day Gilbert was due to take part in *Twenty Questions*. The thought of it unnerved me. But his friend persuaded him to go to bed until it was time to start. Before he wakened him he telephoned for a taxi and, dead on time, the three of us left for the studio in the Paris Cinema in Lower Regent Street, with Gilbert still half asleep. I was certain that he was quite incapable of taking part in a broadcast but, as we neared the studio, he pulled himself together a little, gave me a handful of silver, and told me to take the taxi on to Victoria Station so that I could catch my train home to Penge. I ran all the way home from the station in order to be in time for the start of *Twenty Questions*. I wondered how on earth the announcer would explain Gilbert's absence from the programme. I managed to switch on just in time.

'Well, here we are again with *Twenty Questions*,' said the voice – and it was Gilbert Harding himself, sounding just as he had always sounded on every other programme, just as he had sounded at nine-fifteen that morning, blandly sober at the breakfast-table.

It was my first experience of his astounding ability to pull himself out of his personal difficulties – sickness, intoxication, ill-temper or worry – to produce the Gilbert Harding the public expected to see and hear. As one of his friends once said, 'The public always gets the best of him.'

On my way to work the next morning I was apprehensive. Many times before I had met miserable, growling bears with very sore heads after a night's drinking: this, I felt, would be the biggest, most bad-tempered bear of them all. I was quite wrong.

Gilbert was still in bed, but he showed not the least sign of a hangover. 'I'm a bit tired,' he said. 'I didn't get to bed until six o'clock.' But he was blandly cheerful – and very polite. He was most anxious to be reassured that his behaviour the previous evening hadn't shocked or hurt me. 'I do hope that I wasn't offensive to you,' he said tentatively, and, the incident closed, we turned to the day's work.

He had already opened the morning's mail. There were even more letters than on the previous day. He dictated replies to a few of them, and on the rest he had already pencilled the initials

'N P C' or the words, 'Sorry, no.' N P C meant 'nice post-card'. This was an acknowledgement of fan letters, for which the formula had been given to me the previous day. Occasionally it was possible to vary them slightly to fit particular circumstances, but generally the nice postcards bore the words, 'Thank you very much indeed for your extremely kind and encouraging letter. It was good of you to take the trouble to write and I very much appreciate it.' Sometimes, when there was a delay in answering the fan letters but more often just to relieve the monotony, I would begin by saying, 'Please forgive this delay in acknowledging your kind and encouraging letter . . .' If all the N P Cs I have typed were laid end to end . . . !

The letters marked 'Sorry, no' were invitations. Until his ill health made it impossible there were very few weekends when Gilbert did not travel many miles to open bazaars or garden parties in aid of one good cause or another (he would never agree to attend anything called a 'fayre' because he detested 'olde-tyme' spelling). In winter there were many sales of work and charity auctions. He often said that, because he was paid a great deal of money for doing very little in his job, he felt morally bound to help good causes and charities as much as possible. But he could not, of course, accept all the invitations – there were too many.

I have so often heard it said that some celebrities earn a good part of their income by attending charity functions that I must say that Gilbert Harding was certainly not one of them. He did charge fees – and sometimes very high ones – for opening new shops or showrooms, exhibitions, or any other commercial venture. But never once did he ask for payment of any kind when he attended any event designed to raise money for charity. Occasionally, when he lectured at schools, the local Education Committee insisted on his expenses being paid. In that case the money was always sent to the head of the school with the request that it should be used to buy books for the library.

Most celebrities, I believe, do as he did. But I certainly knew of one star of radio and television, famous for his warm heart and great humanity, who charged very substantial fees when he appeared for charity. He was once asked to open a garden party to raise money for the restoration of an Anglican church in the West Country, and wrote a charming letter of acceptance, adding that his fee would be fifty pounds. The committee secretary wrote back saying that, thanks to the sale of her late husband's stamp collection for just over eighty pounds on behalf of the fund, they would be able to pay the fee. By return of post came another letter from the star, bitterly regretting that his secretary had made a mistake in typing his payment as £50: it should, in fact, have read £75. It was then the star's turn to receive a letter by the next post. The committee, too, regretted the mistake, for they were unable to afford the larger payment and now considered the matter closed.

There was one occasion when Gilbert agreed to act as compère for a big Sunday night charity concert in London. A few days before the concert he was genuinely horrified to receive, from the theatrical agent organizing it, a contract agreeing to pay him seventy-five guineas for his services. Gilbert decided it must be a mistake, but when he telephoned to the agent he was told that all the artists taking part were to be paid. 'In that case,' Harding bellowed into the receiver, 'I withdraw my acceptance. I shall certainly not appear. My name must be removed from the posters at once!' It took the agent a long time and a lot of words to persuade him that it would probably cost more than seventy-five guineas to change everything at the last minute and reprint posters and programmes. So Gilbert agreed to appear. But when the cheque came he immediately endorsed it and sent it to the charity for which the concert had been staged. He never again agreed to do anything of that kind until he had been satisfied that everyone concerned was appearing without a fee.

For many years he was a regular supporter of an annual Sunday night performance given to raise money for theatrical charities, until he quite accidentally discovered that the four stars to whom he had given a lift home in his own hired car after the show had each claimed – and received – 'expenses for hire of car' in sums ranging from four to seven pounds. That was his last appearance for that particular charity organization.

Not only the amount of the daily post surprised me but the variety. His advice and help were sought on almost every conceivable subject; he had letters of obscene abuse as well as of lavish praise; he received mildly flirtatious notes on rose-scented paper, passionate declarations of love briefly written on a postcard or filling a child's exercise book from cover to cover, or blackmailing letters from women who threatened to commit suicide if he would not meet them; admirers sent gifts ranging from hand-knitted tea-pot cosies to sets of antique silver spoons – all of them unsolicited, many of them unwanted and unusable; he received 'readings' from amateur astrologers forecasting a long-lasting and glittering future, and anonymous letters threatening a violent and sudden end.

So I met through the mail people who, during my years as Gilbert's secretary, were to become postal acquaintances of long-standing; people whose foibles and frenzies, problems and pastimes I came to know almost as well as those of my own family. I even made some true friends whom I met through those letters.

But I had yet to meet any of Gilbert's famous colleagues. The first celebrity I spoke to on the telephone was Nancy Spain. She rang to ask if Gilbert was free to lunch with her later that week. He was, and it was arranged that Miss Spain should call at the flat for a drink before going on to lunch. Nancy's telephone voice is as warm and lively as her personality; she sounded charming. I had read and enjoyed many of her books and I was thrilled at the prospect of meeting her. Alas, on the morning of the very day, she telephoned again to say that the *Daily Express* was sending her to North Africa and she had to leave immediately. I was very disappointed. But that charm and her friendliness with my boss were going to cause me a lot of trouble in a few months' time.

Gilbert guessed at my disappointment. When he was in a good mood nothing made him happier than to give pleasure to other people, so I think it was intended as much as a treat for me, as for himself, when he suggested he should invite Hermione Gingold to lunch with us both at a Knightsbridge restaurant. He told me to ring Miss Gingold while he was having his bath. Hermione can never have had a more ardent admirer than I and when I heard her wonderful gravel-and-fur voice, my own voice very nearly left me.

It was already almost one o'clock and Miss Gingold announced that she was 'lunching on a tray'. 'Mr. Harding and his secretary are more than welcome to join me on the tray,' she said, 'but there's very little room – and even less food.' The invitation was declined.

Another time she was invited to come round for a drink before lunch. Miss Gingold said she was about to go out shopping – for a mink coat. She told me that her heart had been broken when her house was ransacked by thieves and her mink coat stolen. 'But,' she added, 'I feel a *leetle* bit better each time I look at the cheque the insurance company have sent me.'

It was many months before I actually met her. She was coming to London for a brief visit after her great success in New York and I went with Gilbert to Waterloo to meet the boat train. The long-delayed meeting had been worth waiting for. At the small 'welcome home' party, given for her by Brian Desmond Hurst, she sparkled with wit and malice in stories of her life in New York.

'And what is Hermione Baddeley doing nowadays?' she asked someone.

'She's touring in *The Diary of a Nobody*.'

'Really!' said Miss G. 'Did she write it herself?'

Only one thing had upset Miss Gingold since she had arrived at Southampton that morning. All the way across the Atlantic she had promised her American friends that she would buy them their first cup of real English tea on the boat train. 'And what do you think we got?' she moaned dramatically. 'Evaporated milk!' Gilbert felt that this was unlikely or inexcusable and he asked me to telephone to his friend Jack Brebner, British Railways' Public Relations Officer, to find out if it could possibly be true. The next day Mr. Brebner's office rang to say that, although fresh milk was normally used in restaurant cars, they had in fact had to use sterilized milk on that particular day. Gilbert asked me to pass the information on to Miss Gingold. 'And that isn't the first time that sterilization has been used to overcome a difficulty,' was her dark comment.

The massive mail, the constant telephone calls, the intricacies of appointments and engagements – gradually I got used to them. I need not, I discovered, have worried about learning the book-keeping or filing systems. Neither of them really existed. Fortunately, Mr. Harding employed excellent accountants and almost the only book-keeping I had to do was, at the end of the year, to send them the receipts, the bank statements, the cheque-book stubs and the bank paying-in book.

Each month I wrote out the cheques, which Gilbert then signed, for the local tradesmen, wine merchants, restaurants and so on, and, as often as I could persuade my employer to endorse them, I paid cheques into the bank. For some extraordinary reason, which I cannot now properly remember, I had been working for him for two months before I was paid. I think it must have been because I was too shy – or felt it would be presumptuous – to write my own salary cheque. Luckily for me, during a signing session one day, Gilbert said, 'That's strange. I can't remember having signed any cheques for you. Have I?' I was never shy about it after that.

But I was quite baffled by the problem of having to deduct my own Pay As You Earn income tax. Arithmetic has never been easy for me and I was sure that the intricacies of the tax tables would defeat me. I was astonished and relieved, when I decided to consult the local tax office, to find how helpful the staff were. When they had explained it to me, I really understood P A Y E. But I was still glad that I had only my own tax to work out – and that only once a month.

For the first few days I carefully made carbon copies of all the letters I typed. Eventually I had quite a pile of copies and felt it was high time to do a little filing, but when I asked Gilbert how he wanted them kept, he was horrified to learn that I had wasted so much time and paper. 'Never keep a copy of anything,' he said. 'Nothing I ever write is of sufficient importance for all that trouble.' This was not, of course, true and often, unknown to him, I took carbon copies of what I considered were important letters. More than once, later, I was glad of it. The filing cabinet, as Gilbert conceived it, was little more than an amplified address book. Most of the letters in it had been put there because the address might be needed; some because their contents were important and notes of his reply had been scribbled in the margin. His method and mine, used together, were very successful and I rarely failed to find what was wanted.

I had been working at Cadogan Place for three or four weeks before I met his mother. Until Gilbert came to live in that furnished flat, he had shared one in Twickenham with his sister, Constance, the headmistress of a local school. Then he had moved to town so that his mother could take his place and be with Constance through her tragic illness and death from cancer. Now Mrs. Harding had decided that she would go and live with her sister in Hereford and was coming to lunch with Gilbert to discuss the move.

Although he and his mother were never at ease together for very long, Gilbert was deeply fond of her. He decided that we would have a really special lunch. In consultation with Mrs. Clarke he planned a meal of asparagus, cold roast duck and salad, followed by strawberries and cream. Neither asparagus nor strawberries were yet in season, so were very expensive indeed. That afternoon Mrs. Clarke cooked the duck and Fortnum and Mason delivered the asparagus, the strawberries and a half-pint bottle of thick Jersey cream, which were put in the refrigerator. That night Gilbert was going to a party so there was no need for an evening meal.

When I arrived for work the following morning there was no sign of Gilbert. For the first time since I had been his secretary, the bedroom door was closed. A few minutes later Mrs. Clarke appeared with a tired and anxious face. 'Oh, dear, Mr. Storey, the lunch,' she wailed. 'There I was downstairs, and suddenly I heard Mr. Harding clattering about in the kitchen above me. There was someone with him and they were both stamping around. About four o'clock it was. I knew what they were after. They must have been looking for some eggs for breakfast and I knew there was only one in the fridge. Then suddenly everything came flying out of the window – the strawberries and the asparagus and the bottle of cream. Thank Heaven he remembered to open the window first!'

I burst out laughing, but Mrs. Clarke was quite serious. A few weeks earlier, she told me, she had been wakened by an inexplicable, dull thump: the following morning she had seen the wall opposite Gilbert's kitchen window decorated with the remains of a large, rich, chocolate cake, which an admirer had sent him the previous day, while a window pane had gaped raggedly. I looked out of the window myself then. The tiled wall was patterned with bright scarlet patches, and thick blobs of cream still clung to the tiles.

But when, after a brief sleep, Gilbert appeared, he was calm, refreshed and in a glowing mood. My fears subsided. When the letters had been dealt with, his mind turned to lunch. 'Come on now, Roger, we had better start. Get the asparagus and the strawberries out of the fridge, will you?' Obviously, the events of the early morning had been completely obliterated from his mind. Fortunately, Mrs. Clarke was at hand in the kitchen to help with the explanations. After one puzzled look, he took it well and simply picked up the telephone to call for replacements to be sent round immediately. One completely blank spot remained in his mind, however. Several times during the morning he plaintively asked, 'But what became of the half-pint of cream we got yesterday?' By the time Mrs. Harding arrived, all was ready for the lunch, just as it had been planned the day before. It was a great success.

I liked Gilbert's mother on sight. She seemed very small and fragile beside him, although she shared with him the inability to suffer fools gladly. It was the only characteristic they had in common, I believe. She was gentle, kind and tolerant. I met her four or five times before she moved to Hereford. We went to Twickenham two or three days in succession to help her to pack up her clothes and the few small pieces of furniture she was taking with her.

A few months later Mrs. Harding came down from Hereford to

stay at Cadogan Place for a fortnight, but it wasn't a particularly happy holiday for her. She was not feeling at all well and I felt that she sensed the lack of sympathy in her son. Like many other vital people, he was always slightly afraid – and even resentful – of illness in others. When he asked, 'How are you?' he never wanted to hear any answer but 'Very well, thank you', and would try to change the subject if anyone started to describe their symptoms. So he was not as attentive or as sympathetic as he might have been. He was naturally out a good deal, fulfilling his normal engagements, and as Mrs. Harding didn't feel like going out, I spent many hours in her company.

Gilbert had always been a great worry to her, she told me. From the time he was a small child he had suffered violent and uncontrollable tempers, which had caused her frequent and prolonged unhappiness. She knew – as indeed everyone did who saw much of him – that he consistently drank too much. She was enormously proud of him and of all that he had achieved. He had been, after all, the child of poor parents – the Master and Matron of the Workhouse at Hereford – and his father had died when he was only four years old. By hard work he had won scholarships, first to the Royal Orphanage at Wolverhampton, and then to Queens' College, Cambridge, where he read Modern Languages. He had been, in turn, a policeman and a school teacher: now he was a journalist and a famous star of sound radio and television.

'But I am afraid,' she said. 'One day, I know, either by drinking or through that unbridled tongue, he will throw it all away. He's been lucky, so far. Somehow, whatever he does or says, he's usually so genuinely sorry afterwards that you always forgive him. Perhaps he has been fortunate too often. Perhaps some day when he says he's sorry, it will be too late.'

She was a woman of great warmth, but her affection was not lightly given. So I was very moved when one day she told me how much she liked me and how grateful she was to me for helping her son. She said that since she had seen how much Gilbert now relied on me, and to what good purpose, she felt happier about him than she had for many years.

'Because I know how incredibly difficult and unkind Gilbert can be,' she said, 'I'm not going to ask you to *promise* anything, but I am asking that, when the time comes – as it surely will – when you feel you can't stand working for him any longer, you will think very seriously and then, if necessary, think again before taking the final step.' I assured her that, just as I had not lightly taken on the job, I would not lightly abandon it.

A few days after this conversation, Mrs. Harding returned to Hereford. Because Gilbert was never a very good correspondent, she asked me if I would write to her from time to time and tell her truthfully what he was doing. We exchanged several letters, but I never saw her again. She died a few months after her stay at Cadogan Place.

On the day Mrs. Harding came to lunch on strawberries and asparagus we ate in the dining-room – my office. Fortunately, this did not often happen for before the dining-table could be used for its proper purpose, a great deal of clearing up had to be done. It was always piled with books, papers, letters and stationery. The clearing up was not nearly so difficult as the subsequent sorting out. Mrs. Clarke's method of making room for a meal was quick and effective – everything was swept off in armfuls and dumped in one pile in a corner. The result, for me, was days of chaos.

Gilbert really enjoyed having people to lunch, but in those days the food was usually quite simple. He liked pottering about in the kitchen himself but at Cadogan Place Mrs. Clarke did most of the cooking. It was usually fried fish, grilled steak or cutlets – 'small, lean cutlets, not sleazy, greasy mutton chops' he would insist. A chicken, a joint, or boiled beef and carrots – his favourite dish for many years – were served when he was feeling ambitious.

For some time before I became his secretary, Gilbert had been writing his life story. It had been commissioned as a serial by the magazine *John Bull*, and they had made available to him the services of an experienced journalist, Charles Hamblett. Whenever he could manage a few hours at a time, Gilbert dictated the story to him. It was then written up and the manuscript sent back for G.H.'s approval or correction. Frequently, he would leave London on Friday to work with Hamblett at a quiet hotel in the Isle of Wight, and return on Sunday in time for *What's My Line?*

One Thursday afternoon, when I was alone in the flat, a newspaperman telephoned to say that they had heard rumours of an incident in which Mr. Harding had been involved, in an Isle of Wight public house. Before printing the story they would like confirmation from Mr. Harding himself. I was taken completely by surprise and was able to say, quite truthfully, that I knew nothing of any 'incident'. I did my best to combine bland ignorance and shocked amazement in my answer. But the suggestion worried me. A few minutes later came a call from another newspaper. They, too, had heard the rumour – but in greater detail. The incident, according to their version, involved the exchange of blows between Gilbert and a woman. When could they talk to Mr. Harding about it? Before Gilbert came back, almost every national daily and London evening newspaper had heard some kind of story and detailed a man to check it. The telephone rang continuously. And still I was able to stave them off with a protestation of innocence.

By now I was used to regular calls from newspaper reporters or television and radio feature writers, seeking information about the programmes in which he appeared or checking on some detail of his day-to-day routine or engagements. This was the first time I had had to face an obviously hostile press in full cry after a scandal. My total ignorance was a wonderful shield.

When, in the evening, Gilbert returned, he told me exactly what had happened. After a tiring day's work on the book, he and Hamblett had decided to relax at the local. In the bar was a rather drunken woman, with a strong Irish accent, who not only recognized him but, again and again, tried to draw him into conversation. Three times she called on the barman to 'give Gilbert Harding a drink with me!' Three times, growing more and more angry, he refused. The fourth time he lost patience, self-control and discretion. 'Get back to the dirty ditches of Dublin, you dreary, drooling drab!' he cried. Not surprisingly, the lady slapped his face. Gilbert slapped back. The landlord persuaded the woman to leave the bar and Gilbert finished his drink in peace before returning to his hotel and to bed.

He had barely finished telling me the story when the telephone rang again. He answered it himself. Yet another newspaper reporter was checking. I shrank into myself with dismay as I heard Gilbert reply 'I have no comment to make'. There was a second call. He answered with the same words. Tentatively I suggested that 'no comment' was not the best reply: it implied that there might be more than rumour in the story. 'Wouldn't it be better,' I suggested, 'if I go on answering the telephone and pretending that you are still out and I know nothing either of the incident or of when you will be back?' He agreed and for the rest of the day I continued to stonewall – in some cases two or three times to the same reporter.

In those days Gilbert subscribed to Finders Limited. If you were to be out, all incoming telephone calls would automatically be put through to them and they would take messages. When I left that evening, all I had to do was to ring the exchange and refer all calls to Finders. That took care of the newspapers for about fourteen hours. Innocently, I assumed that, after that time, the rumour would have died.

The next morning, when I reached the flat, I cancelled the switch-over and rang Finders. They relayed dozens of newspaper inquiries – all of them eagerly begging Mr. Harding to be so kind as to ring back. So it continued. All that day the urgent calls came in. Again and again and again I answered, 'I'm sorry. Mr. Harding is out and I don't know when he will be back.' I was deeply sympathetic towards the unhappy reporters – I could so well imagine their exasperation with my mock sorrow. I knew that they knew that I knew that no newspaper dare print such a story without incontrovertible evidence. And it seemed obvious that such evidence was lacking.

Then my confidence was shaken. From the *Daily Telegraph* – which I had always considered to be the second most sedate and unsensational of the national dailies – came two telegrams within an hour. The second was reply-paid and said that unless they could discuss the matter with Mr. Harding they proposed to print the story 'as received' the following day. It took a great deal of courage – and quite a lot of harrowing discussion – before we both agreed to ignore it.

That was quite late in the afternoon. There were no more telephone calls but no work was done. Mr. Harding realized as well as I did that if such a story, sensationally presented, were to appear in an influential newspaper – 'Television Star Slaps Fan' – it would be a formidable check to his career.

I didn't normally take the *Daily Telegraph,* but the following morning I was outside the newsagent's shop as it opened and had skimmed every page before I got to Cadogan Place. When I reached the flat, I found that Gilbert had done the same. But there was no mention at all of the incident – not in the *Daily Telegraph* or any other daily newspaper. And that was the last we heard of it. Our patient stonewalling had won a notable victory.

Perhaps victory is not the right word from the point of view of the public who had created the Gilbert Harding legend. But we certainly thought it was. To any well-known figure the press can be friend or enemy – but one can never be sure of its mood.

I gradually learned to be on my guard when I answered reporters' inquiries. Usually all they wanted was details of radio or television programmes in which Gilbert was taking part. Sometimes, because of either policy or ignorance, I could not give them the answer, for I had soon learned that it was better to say nothing until I was certain of the facts.

One reporter asked me who was appearing with Gilbert in a forth-coming programme and I answered that I thought so-and-so would be in it. The next morning his column carried the story that Mr. Harding's secretary had given this information. In fact, not only had so-and-so not been asked, but no one had even thought of inviting him to take part. I had to do a great deal of explaining to a lot of people.

But, perhaps because of my sympathy for the harassed newspaper-man in his constant battle with deadlines, space, editors and sub-editors, I learned to have patience with the frequent misquotations or misrepresentations of my answers. The oddest misquotation occurred when one of the London evening papers rang to ask about Mr. Harding's part in a television programme the following evening.

'Mr. Harding is in Blackpool, where he is to switch on the illu-minations tonight,' I said. 'But he will have to catch a train at the crack of dawn tomorrow to get to the studio in time for the rehearsal.' Then, catching myself in an exaggeration, I added, 'Well, perhaps the second crack of dawn.'

The newspaper announced, pompously, 'Tomorrow, says Gilbert Harding's secretary, he will awaken to the crack of the second dawn.'

Gilbert himself was, on the whole, co-operative with the press. At the time when he was in Cyprus, primarily as a schoolmaster, he had also worked as a correspondent for *The Times* and so always looked on himself to some extent as a working journalist even before his popularity as a radio star made him a sought-after columnist. He realized, therefore, that reporters had a job to do and, except for occasional outbursts of furious impatience, was prepared to help them do it.

So it became apparent, very early in my job, that the title 'private secretary' was a misnomer. The secretary to a public figure, I learned, had to be a 'public secretary' too. In fact, the job constantly revealed new and unexpected aspects.

At the end of my first week, in spite of my efforts, we still seemed to have arrears of correspondence and, because Gilbert was to be away from London on the following Monday and Tuesday, I suggested that it might be helpful if I came in to work on the Saturday morning. With enthusiastic expressions of gratitude, he accepted my offer. The following week the same thing happened. I am quite sure that it was in no way intentional but, after that, Gilbert would invariably say, on Friday afternoon, 'In the morning we really must deal with this, that or the other.' And I was much too shy – or weak or foolish or stupid – to say, 'It's Saturday tomorrow and I shan't be here.' So, for one reason and another, almost two years went by before I finally got around to establishing the fact that I had not been engaged to work on Saturdays at all, let alone until two or three in the afternoon.

Then came Tai-Mu. And I really began to realize that I was part of the Harding household.

One day Billy Thatcher, one of the scriptwriters of *Mrs. Dale's Diary*, had asked Gilbert if he would write a foreword to his book about Tai-Lu, the Siamese cat who had already become a popular character on television's *Children's Hour*. Gilbert, who had seen the programmes and loved them, read the book and enjoyed it enormously. He wrote just the kind of foreword Billy had hoped for.

In doing so he apparently stimulated his own feelings. He wanted a Siamese kitten. And without delay. Billy Thatcher was asked if he knew where we could buy one but that, it seemed, was out of the question. Tai-Lu had recently had kittens and he would be very hurt if Gilbert would not accept one of them as a gift. So Tai-Mu was delivered the next day. She became part of my job, too.

She was a delightful creature – shy, but lively, with a voice quite out of proportion to her tiny, angular frame. Tai-Mu couldn't bear to be left alone for a second. Quite a lot of the time she slept and then it didn't matter, but the moment she woke she demanded company. If she didn't get it she cried and cried and cried, at the top of her poignant voice. Since Gilbert was out most of the day, Mrs. Clarke and I became responsible for her welfare. At first she liked to sit on my knee while I worked, but then she decided it would be more comfortable on my shoulder. She took to climbing up and draping herself round my neck.

She did not like the clatter of the typewriter but that did not drive her from her chosen position. She just mewed her protests in my ear. But she hated the telephone bell. Each time it rang, she jumped in alarm and dug her needle-sharp claws into my shoulder to save herself from falling. I didn't mind when she dug them into my coat collar, but, more often than not, the claws missed my collar and found my neck.

For most of the day, however, she managed to relax. It was when Gilbert came home that she really woke up. She leaped from chair-back to chair-back, streaked up one curtain, along the pelmet and down the other. She jumped to Gilbert's knee, raced over his shoulder, became airborne and landed in a slither of falling papers on the polished table, from which she skidded to the floor. He used to take her basket into his bedroom at night and sometimes she continued her gymnastics there, while he tried vainly to sleep. More than once – in spite of the trays of turf-and-soil which were scattered all over the flat – she used one of his shoes for her last 'potty' of the night.

My neck was constantly lacerated with Tai-Mu's terror: there wasn't a scrap of upholstery in the flat which didn't show signs of her athletic displays and Gilbert was growing hollow-eyed from lack of sleep. At a final, sad conference, we decided that she must return home. I took her back to St. John's Wood in a taxi. She cried heart-rendingly all the way and I felt almost like a murderer. But when I saw her pleasure and excitement at the reunion with her mother and father and her brothers and sisters, when she left me without a backward glance or a farewell wail, my conscience was at rest.

I had worked at Cadogan Place for about eight weeks when I went to France for my summer holiday. Until then I had been willing to believe that a change was as good as a rest. The last eight weeks had been a great change for me – but now I needed the rest. I had seen my employer in every conceivable mood: serious, sentimental, gay, overbearing, open-handed, grim, serene, furious – and drunk. I had coped with situations which, two months earlier, I could not have imagined myself either being faced with or having to face. I had had to deal with him slightly drunk and rather querulous; very drunk, quarrelsome and malicious; dead drunk and incoherent. Of the three stages, I already knew that I preferred the last. All I had to do then was to help him into bed, or make him as comfortable as possible in any chair he flopped into, and leave sleep and nature to do the rest.

The last day before my holiday had been more than usually difficult. Gilbert had returned from lunch in the middle stage. There were many things to discuss and several telephone messages to give him. But nothing I said or did seemed to meet with approval. He wouldn't sign the letters I had typed. He wouldn't dictate replies to the letters still unanswered. And he continued to drink large brandy-and-sodas until eventually he reached the third stage. Finally – and almost in despair – I decided that the only thing to do was to type a long list of all the things I had been trying to tell him all the afternoon and leave it where he would find it the following morning.

By the time I left Cadogan Place and my snoring boss, it was the early hours of Saturday morning. I got home, did my packing and had only three hours' sleep before I had to leave for the airport.

The first few days of my holiday were haunted by the recurring memory of all that had been left undone and unsaid before I left, but then I began to relax and enjoy myself. On the last night I sat drinking with friends on the terrace of an hotel overlooking the main square at St. Malo. From my schooldays I had always hated the last day of any holiday, but the hollow feeling inside me that night was more than the usual end-of-holiday feeling. I just did not want to go back to my new job. I could honestly say that I did not for one moment regret that I had accepted it: but how I wished that I had never had the chance to!

CHAPTER THREE

MAKING HEADLINES

THE enormous piles of letters which I found waiting after my holiday did not cheer me up. But Gilbert did. He seemed so genuinely pleased to see me, so delighted that I had enjoyed my trip, that I soon found myself wondering how I could possibly have dreaded my return to Cadogan Place.

This was to be the pattern of my feelings for all the years I worked for Gilbert Harding. Sometimes, for days on end, when his moodiness, his outbursts of bad temper, or drunken scenes shattered my nerves and my spirit, I would wonder how much longer I could stand it. I would long for the courage to give him my notice. Then, suddenly, the whole situation would change. For days – sometimes for weeks – at a time his mood would be sunny, reasonable and endearing. During those periods I would not have changed jobs with anyone in the world.

Except when Gilbert was away, or when he had an early morning engagement, we spent the first couple of hours each morning going through the day's mail. By this time he dictated very little for I was able to deal with most of the correspondence with little reference to him. But my typing could, in the main, only be done when he was out or had visitors. He could not bear to be alone for very long, so, if he was at home and had no friends in, or if he wasn't in the mood for work we spent many hours just sitting and talking. He was always immensely interested in the detail of people's experience and enjoyed asking questions about my life before I had worked for him – the theatre, the publishing house, my sister and her family, my parents in Yorkshire – he was interested in everything. I must admit, too, that when I ran out of suitable anecdotes, I invented a few.

Fortunately for my work, Gilbert had a great many engagements

that summer. He had to make regular appearances at a Bournemouth hotel, where he introduced the cabaret. It was not a role
he enjoyed, but the fee he was paid for these brief appearances
handsomely compensated him for the discomfort. Now that *What's
My Line?* was resting for the summer, he was free to accept weekend
engagements. For five weekends in succession he visited the Butlin
holiday camps – Skegness, Filey, Clacton, Pwllheli and the hotel at
Saltdean – where he acted as chairman for a programme of *Twenty
Questions*, the team being recruited from the visitors and the camp
staffs.

One Sunday he went to Leicester for a stage presentation of
What's My Line? in the de Montfort Hall; he made guest appearances at Sunday night concerts in towns as far apart as Clacton,
Colwyn Bay and Bolton; during the week he opened exhibitions
at Manchester, Eastbourne and Burnley; he took part in a Brains
Trust at Sheffield and again at Liverpool, sandwiching in the
opening of a factory extension at Sunderland. But, whatever else
happened, he had to be in London each Thursday to write his
weekly column for *The People* and to take part in the *Twenty
Questions* broadcasts.

When I went to work for him, Gilbert had already been writing
weekly for *The People* for over a year. It had started through an
article written in that paper by Kenneth Baily, the radio critic.
Mr. Baily had, it seemed, got rather tired of hearing Gilbert's
continuous grievances. In an article headed *A Challenge to Radio's
Gas-Bag – Really, Mr. Harding, it's about Time you DID Something!* he challenged Gilbert to come out and set about righting
some of the wrongs he grumbled of. Gilbert constantly maintained
that as long as people sat back and accepted second-rate conditions,
bullying officialdom and bad service, they could never hope for
anything better. Mr. Baily said that throughout the country there
were many thousands of people who, because of ignorance, old age,
ill health or just fear, were unable to fight their own battles with
authority. He challenged Gilbert to take up the cudgels on their
behalf instead of just talking about it.

I imagine a lot of *People* readers – perhaps Kenneth Baily himself – were surprised when Gilbert accepted the challenge. The
newspaper announced that he would be interested to hear from its
readers who had any such problems. The letters flooded in. They
came from people in abysmal housing conditions, from disabled
ex-servicemen longing for work, from those who felt entitled to a

pension they could not get, from people who considered they had
been swindled, from parents who could not get help for a mentally
afflicted child – from men and women, young and old, well and
sick, with a complaint of some sort, mostly reasonable and many
capable of an easy solution. Some of them were so pathetically
simple that they only needed a brief letter to put them right: some
were so complex that it needed weeks of work by experts to
straighten them out. Gilbert, with Kenneth Baily, travelled all over
the country, satisfying himself that he was dealing with genuine
cases, battling with local housing officers, sanitary inspectors, medical officers, builders and hire-purchase shops. Each Sunday he
printed the story of his journeys and of some of the people he had
tried to help.

The People office was deluged with pleas for his help. It was
absolutely impossible for him to deal with more than a small
percentage of them himself, so reporters and investigators were
drafted to help him. *The People*'s Free Advice Bureau was working
overtime. Indeed, they still answer hundreds of such letters every
week.

But when the winter came, the strain of all this travelling in
cold, and sometimes foggy, weather, began to affect Gilbert's health.
The mild form of asthma, from which he had suffered for some
time, became more and more troublesome and after a few months
he could no longer manage the journeys. It would have been easier
if he had been able to spend a few days in each place he had to
visit, but it had all to be done at high speed because he was obliged
to return to London almost every other day to keep up his other
commitments. Little by little *The People* reporters took over the
job and their reports were sent to Gilbert in London, where he
dealt with other problems by telephone and letter.

For several months his weekly article in *The People* was based
on these investigations, but gradually it took on a more general
theme. The editor of the newspaper was pleased with the increase
in readership that his efforts had brought and invited him to
become a regular columnist. Gilbert was delighted to be able to
call himself a journalist again.

Every Thursday, then, he went to the Long Acre offices of *The
People* to dictate his column to the editor's secretary. Occasionally,
if his health or his engagements made it difficult for him to go there,
Kate Wadleigh would come to take the dictation at Cadogan Place
and sometimes stay to lunch with us. Over the years Kate became

a close friend of his – and of mine. Like me, she had to answer on his behalf many of the letters from enthusiastic readers which swelled *The People* mail. Like me, she learned to know Gilbert's varying moods and failing health, for, in later years, she had to take dictation often beside a hospital bed.

Although I had been to *What's My Line?* once or twice with Gilbert it wasn't until he was asked to do a programme called *A Little of What You Fancy,* in mid-August 1953, that I had my first real experience of a television studio. The programme was based on his personal likes and dislikes and was very varied. It included a discussion on good and bad party-giving between himself and Barbara Back – a colleague on *The People*; conjuring by Tommy Cooper; poetry read by Robert Harris; various items of music; a demonstration of flower arrangement by the late Constance Spry; and Philip Harben teaching Gilbert how to cook an omelette. Conferences on the programme had been started in July, but for two weeks before it began, the producer Bill Ward and many of the people taking part were constant and often day-long visitors to Cadogan Place.

It was the first time the B B C had allowed Gilbert to give rein to his own ideas. He was excited, persuasive, modest and exceedingly anxious to please. One morning I arrived to find him striding about the office, script in hand. 'Roger,' he cried, waving the typescript at me, 'this could be the beginning of something different – something with a bit of life in it. It might save me from an eternity of being nothing but a piddling panel puppet!' I muttered something and kept my fingers crossed. I just hoped that his determination would last out the week before the show went on.

On the Monday and Tuesday mornings he had to report at a film studio for his part – a very small one – in a film being made for American television networks. He went straight from the film studio to Lime Grove for rehearsals, which continued all day Wednesday. On Thursday morning, rehearsals again, an appearance as guest of honour at a lunch at the Savoy Hotel and back for more rehearsals. Early that evening he had to return to the flat to be interviewed by Beverley Nichols for an article for a woman's magazine. Then followed the usual *Twenty Questions* broadcast and, after it was off the air, the team recorded a further programme to be broadcast later in the year when they would all be on holiday.

He had a long-standing engagement, that Friday, to open the Royal Horticultural Society's annual Exhibition at the Aberdeen Music

Hall. So, when the second *Twenty Questions* was over, he had to race back to Cadogan Place, pick up an overnight bag and catch the night train to the north. And how he *loathed* the sleeping compartments of trains. He maintained that he found it impossible to breathe in them, much less sleep. But after a strenuous official day in Aberdeen, he had to travel back overnight again to be at the Lime Grove television studios for rehearsal at ten o'clock on Saturday morning.

When I reached the flat that morning, he had been home for two hours, had had breakfast and was ready to leave for the studio. I had expected a bedraggled, ill-slept, unshaven, bad-tempered bear. Instead, he was cheerful and eager. 'Better come with me,' he said, before I had had time to take off my coat.

It was the first whole day I had ever spent in a television studio. It was, I felt, an experience that would last me for a long time. The lights, even for rehearsals without cameras, were at least ten times hotter than any I had experienced as an actor in a film studio. The noise was deafening. The performers were apparently aimless. I just could not believe that any kind of presentable programme could possibly come out of this slatternly confusion. The two non-professionals – Barbara Back and Constance Spry – were not to come until the evening 'because they might lose their spontaneity', said Bill Ward. But everyone else worked almost without a break all day, in a set which was a rough copy of Gilbert's sitting-room at Cadogan Place.

One of his 'dislikes' in the programme was to be potted aspidistras. Two of these, in elaborate pots on stands, decorated the set and Bill had planned that Gilbert was to pick them up and hurl them towards – but just missing – the cameras. Twice, at rehearsal, he underestimated his strength and the aspidistras flew over the camera-crew's heads, missing them by a fraction of an inch.

In presenting one of his favourite gramophone records to the viewers, Gilbert was to be seen actually putting it on the radiogram. The machine worked perfectly to cue during rehearsal. During the transmission, he had to coax it for what seemed like several minutes before any sound at all was heard. But the item before the record had been Tommy Cooper's act, so perhaps the breakdown didn't seem to be unintentional to the viewers. For Tommy Cooper's conjuring tricks, as always, failed to work out. Each one always ended in something utterly unexpected and quite miraculous, which filled him, as well as his audience, with astonishment. For one trick, Tommy had asked Gilbert to hold a large jug of water on his head.

'Now stand very, very still, because I'm going to turn that water into wine and we mustn't spill a drop, must we, Gilbert?' He didn't spill a drop. Somehow, magically, a whole cascade of wine poured down Gilbert's face and across his dinner-jacket and white dress shirt. There was a small audience in the studio for the performance and, when this happened, there was an audible gasp of pleasurable anticipation. They were quite certain that they were going to hear an 'In Person' display of Gilbert's well-publicised fury. Instead, he beamed through the rivulets of wine.

The next day – Sunday – the newspapers showed that the television critics were by no means enthusiastic about his programme. Some coldly admitted to having been bored. But the B B C had already reported many telephone messages of congratulation and hundreds of letters from delighted viewers were to follow the next day. But Gilbert had no time to consider the critics' views, he had to appear in Clacton at a Sunday concert. On Monday he travelled to Hereford to spend three days with his mother and then back to London on Thursday for his *People* article and *Twenty Questions*. Friday was spent in making an advertising film for cigarettes and on the Saturday he travelled to Bournemouth for his appearance as compère of the cabaret.

The first three days of the following week were spent on the film again and on the Saturday he was to travel to Bridlington for a concert on the Sunday. All his spare time between these engagements was spent working on his life story for *John Bull*. And there were still letters from fans, begging letters, requests for appearances, invitations to lunches and dinners to be dealt with, telephone calls to answer, decisions to be made.

So I was not surprised, when I arrived on the Thursday morning, to find him looking grey and tired. I asked him if he was not well. 'I'm all right. Just had a bad night, that's all. Nothing to worry about. Let's get on . . .' he said gruffly. He agreed to dictate his *People* column at home, instead of going out, but throughout the dictation he was constantly interrupted by bouts of coughing. By the evening he felt so unwell that he agreed to call the doctor. He was told that he was grossly over-tired and advised that it would be exceedingly unwise to keep any engagement for the next few days since he was in need of a complete rest. Reluctantly, Gilbert agreed that I should telephone to his agent and cancel his appearance at Bridlington. Above all things, he hated not to fulfil an engagement he had made. To cancel one only added to his nervous distress.

However, this time he did just as he was told – for one day. All Friday, he lay in bed, calling every few minutes 'What's going on, Roger?' wanting to be told who was calling on the telephone, who had rung the doorbell. I was just beginning to think of tidying the desk and going home, when there was a sudden, delighted cry from the bedroom. 'Roger, *I* know! *I* know what I'll do. Come here, quickly!'

I rushed into the room. 'I can't stand this gloomy room and the telephone bell and the doorbell and all the rustle and bustle and hustle. I'll get away. Come on – get the telephone book. Look up the airway's number. I'll fly to Le Touquet. That'll do me more good than frowsting here in bed.'

My protests were useless. He telephoned to a friend in the B B C and persuaded him to go too. He booked two air tickets, packed an overnight bag and flew from Croydon airport early on Saturday morning.

I was pounding away at the typewriter when, the following Monday afternoon, they boisterously returned, flamboyantly influenced by duty-free liquor on the homeward plane. Gilbert did look much more rested than when I had seen him the previous Friday, though, from his account, rest was the last thing he had sought on his brief holiday. But he did look a little strange. After a moment, I realized that his upper lip was swollen and that a single surgical stitch was almost hidden by his moustache. He showed no reluctance to explain. There were, in fact, he said, three stitches. He and his friend had been in a bar until the early hours of Sunday morning and an Englishman and his wife had got into conversation with them. The woman had very strong and very contradictory views on some of the statements Gilbert had made and, in perhaps rather colourful language, he had told her to be quiet. Her husband challenged Gilbert to repeat the remark – and he did, word for word. The man immediately ('and very properly,' said Gilbert) lashed out, hit Gilbert on the mouth and cut his lip with the signet ring he was wearing. The cut bled lavishly and finally a doctor had to be brought to attend to the wound. The following morning the insulted lady had been awakened by a messenger with an enormous bouquet of flowers and one of Gilbert's notes of handsome apology. She had reacted exactly as Mrs. Harding had told me most people reacted to Gilbert's apologies – she accepted the flowers with thanks and the apology with forgiveness. The incident, was, everyone thought, closed. Gilbert's own doctor removed the stitches a few days later and, although he had been afraid the swelling might affect his speech, it didn't, and his moustache hid the scar.

On the evening of Gilbert's return from Le Touquet, I had met Nancy Spain for the first time. She had telephoned soon after his arrival and was invited round for a drink. I had often spoken to her on the telephone, but had formed quite the wrong impression of her. She was much younger and very much more attractive than I had expected. She is one of the easiest people to talk to I have ever met, not only because her conversation is exhilarating but also because the great warmth of her character is so immediately apparent. On that occasion – as on nearly every one, whether at the Caprice, the Dorchester or the Ritz – Nancy wore slacks.

Some months later, a friend who had never met Miss Spain, asked me, in Gilbert's presence, to describe her. 'She is the only distinguished woman author and journalist to be dressed exclusively by the Army Surplus Stores,' I said. Gilbert laughed enormously and later, when one day she was lunching with us, he repeated the description to Nancy. 'But I wish I could remember who said it.' I studied my plate closely and prayed that he wouldn't. 'Oh yes, of course,' he said. 'It was Roger!' Nancy was so delighted with the description that she asked my permission to repeat it in one of her articles.

The night she came for drinks she brought her friend, Joan Werner Laurie, later editor of *She,* with her, and they were treated to a gramophone recital. Gilbert's record-player was a constant pleasure to him – though often not to others. Although he was not tone deaf you would have thought so from the way he used it. There was never any adjustment of treble or bass and the volume control was turned up so that the gramophone itself and every ornament in the room quivered and rattled. To make matters worse, he usually roared out the words of the songs at the limit of his lungs. Any kind of conversation was impossible, and sometimes I couldn't be sure of hearing the telephone ring.

That night it was *Guys and Dolls.* A few weeks earlier Gilbert had been taken to see that American musical at the Coliseum and had been enchanted with it. By the middle of the following morning, the records of the show had been ordered and delivered, and for the next week or two, whenever he was at home, they were played non-stop. After two days, I was word-perfect in every lyric. They were played afresh for every visitor, so, to the accompaniment of a bottle of champagne, on they went again for Nancy and Joan. Then, among others, he played a new favourite of his – *Plus Bleu que tes Yeux*, sung by Patachou. Nancy loved it and, although he had had it for only a few days, Gilbert immediately gave it to her.

Months later, when writing of her great 'romance' with Gilbert, Nancy told her readers that he had once presented her with a gramophone record and that her friends had all thought it to be of the deepest significance. They had seen the title on the other side of the record. It was *Mon Homme* . . . 'My Man'.

That was on the Monday. Two days later, the effect of his disobedience to doctor's orders became apparent. He felt tired and ill. Nevertheless, he insisted on keeping a long-made promise to appear in a stage version of *What's My Line?* at the Battersea Pleasure Gardens in aid of the N S P C C. The following day, in spite of a rising temperature, he made a personal appearance at the Radio Show at Earls Court and took part in a recording there of *Twenty Questions* to be broadcast that evening.

By the time the programme went on the air, Gilbert was in bed and the doctor had been called in. He was told that he must stay in bed for at least a week and the early editions of the evening papers on Friday carried headlines saying 'Gilbert Harding has Bronchitis', 'Harding Ordered to Rest', 'Gilbert Harding "Exhausted" '. I had to cancel his Bournemouth cabaret, the opening of a fête in aid of Harrow Hospital, a Sunday night concert in North Wales, *Twenty Questions* and the opening of exhibitions in Newcastle and Sunderland – a week's work.

He really was exhausted and that, with his temperature, made him doze most of Friday and Saturday. So there seemed little possibility of my getting away at lunch-time that day . . . fortunately, as it happened. When a telephone call came, in the early evening, from a *Sunday Express* reporter, I supposed it to be the normal inquiry about Mr. Harding's health. But it wasn't.

'We understand,' said the reporter, 'that Mr. Harding was involved in a brawl in a Le Touquet night club some time ago. Our information is that he had some injury to his mouth which required medical attention. I wonder if you could confirm that? It seems to have happened during the August Bank Holiday weekend – or was it at Whitsuntide?'

The diary was on the table beside the telephone. I leafed through it quickly and reeled off the list of engagements throughout the Whitsuntide weekend and again over the three days of the August

Bank Holiday. 'So you see,' I said blandly, 'it was quite impossible for Mr. Harding to have fitted in even an afternoon at Le Touquet on either weekend.'

Gilbert had overheard my side of the conversation, so it was not possible to keep the news from him that someone had tipped off the press. We both felt sure that my innocent reply had only staved off inquiries for the time being, and that we should hear more of it. We were right. Within an hour, a *Sunday Express* reporter rang the doorbell. I firmly asserted that Gilbert was much too ill to be interviewed and repeated my denial of the Le Touquet story. After I had got rid of him there were more phone calls and two more visits from the reporter. It was nearly midnight when the last call came through and I still stuck — word for word as far as possible — to my original denial. After that, nothing. It was far too dangerous a story to be printed without confirmation, so, in fact, it never was.

But the threat hung over us for several days and did nothing to improve Gilbert's health since the telephone rang constantly with inquiries about his condition or good wishes for his recovery. His fan mail trebled overnight. Telegrams poured in, and Mrs. Clarke was kept constantly busy opening the door to receive great baskets of fruit and bouquets of flowers. There were so many flowers that we soon ran out of vases and finally had to resort to buckets, camouflaged with leaves and greenery. It was a great relief when we found that the most magnificent bouquet of all — from Anna Neagle and Herbert Wilcox — arrived already arranged in its own pot!

Although Gilbert was feeling too tired and too ill to do anything but stay in bed, his temper did not relax with his body. I, too, was soon exhausted. Once I left him peacefully sleeping and went back to my office to try to deal with a few of the hundreds of letters that needed to be acknowledged. I had closed his bedroom door so that the sound of the clacking typewriter in the next room should not disturb him. But every ten or fifteen minutes I tiptoed in to make sure that he was still sleeping and needed nothing.

A friend was expected to tea that afternoon and, while I was actually in his room checking that he was still not awake, the doorbell rang. I paused for a moment to see if it had awakened him, then, because Mrs. Clarke was out, went to answer the bell. I showed the visitor into the sitting-room and told her that Gilbert was sleeping. Naturally, she begged me not to disturb him for a few minutes, since she had arrived early. We had chatted for perhaps five minutes when the telephone rang. To my complete stupefaction, it was Gilbert's voice I heard as I picked it up. He roared with fury.

'You abandoned me; you selfish, creeping creature!' he yelled. 'I've been awake for an hour, calling and calling. And nobody answered. Nobody gave a curse whether I was alive or dead. Just shut yourself away and don't care. I might be choking to death, for all the trouble you take . . .'

In sheer desperation, he said, he had, on his extension, asked the telephone exchange to put in a test call to our number. Then he had listened for it to ring and when it stopped, as I picked it up, he had lifted his own receiver. I hurried to his bedroom. As I opened the door, the fury burst out again. 'But,' I protested, 'you can't have been awake for much more than five minutes. I was in your room less than ten minutes ago and you were sound asleep.' 'How dare you call me a liar?' Gilbert roared and, with more energy than he had shown for days, hurled at me in quick succession three or four books, the telephone and a jug of barley water. The books missed my head by several inches; the telephone flew only to the length of its cord and then thudded heavily to the floor; the jug of barley water emptied itself mainly into Gilbert's slippers.

Peace and order were restored in time for the visitor to be shown into a tidy room to share the poor invalid's pot of tea. But in the course of the next few days, Gilbert must have asked at least twenty times why his slippers were damp!

A few days later, a van arrived from the Times library with his new library books. There were two due for return but I was not certain that Gilbert had finished them, so I took them into his bedroom to ask him. They were grabbed from my hand. 'The fools!' he bawled. 'The raving, flaming idiots! I had these two books last week. Why, in heaven's name, did you let the van go, you dolt?'

So far, I had not had a chance to say a word. Now I explained, calmly, quietly and in very simple words that two new books were waiting for him in the hall but, before returning the old ones, I just needed to know if he had read them. 'Don't you dare adopt that tone of voice with me . . .' and, once again, books were flying through the air in my direction. Once again they missed me. He was, luckily, always a rotten shot.

It is amusing to tell these stories now. I was not amused at the time. Gilbert in a towering rage was an awe-inspiring sight. I had not known him then for very long and I won't pretend that I wasn't frightened of him.

A corner of the Brighton
house.

(Photo. J. F. Smith, Brighton)

At Brighton with his
cousin's daughters, Sally
(*left*) and Rosalind Bernard.
Sham-pu in the middle.

Attending a wedding with the author.

On holiday in Killarney. Behind the driver is Joan Smith, Gilbert Harding's housekeeper.

A discussion with the late Aneurin Bevan.

All that week I arrived at Cadogan Place at nine o'clock each morning and never got home until well after midnight. Mrs. Clarke attended to his needs between those hours. Apart from dealing with one or two important letters and dictating his article for *The People* from his bed, Gilbert did not work at all that week, but, as he began to feel better, his impatience increased. He was overjoyed when the weekend came and he was allowed to go out once more. He was sunny and kind and over and over again, told us how grateful he was for our care of him and how ashamed of his fractiousness.

One of the things about being allowed out that most pleased him was that he was able to fulfil an engagement which he had been afraid the doctor would forbid. He had been very proud to be asked to make a broadcast appeal on the Sunday night in 'The Week's Good Cause' for the Wireless for the Bedridden Society and had hated the thought that he might not be able to do so. But, although he was not completely fit, he was at Broadcasting House as planned, and his appeal brought the Society over seven thousand pounds. Two years later, taking the place of the late Lord Horder – who had died only a few weeks earlier – Gilbert made a second appeal which raised even more money for the same Society.

The next few weeks were again as busy as they had been before his illness. He had engagements in many parts of the country, spent a few days at Hereford with his mother and was photographed a hundred times, from every possible angle, for his effigy in wax which Tussaud's had finally persuaded him to let them make. In addition he spent two days at Bradford and one at Cambridge being photographed for illustrations for the *John Bull* serialization of his life story.

He was still working hard on this and had been obliged to add several thousand extra words because, rather against his wishes, he had been persuaded to sell to a publisher the rights in a book to be published the following November. His reluctance to do such a book was because he quite genuinely thought that no one would want to buy it. 'People who buy books don't want to read about me. Why on earth should they? Nothing interesting has ever happened to me and I've never done anything important.' But, as publication showed, he was wrong. The book sold steadily and well and was chosen by one of the Book Clubs. It was printed in a paper-back edition, serialized by several provincial newspapers and, with the author himself reading extracts, was serialized in a B B C sound radio programme.

C

Early in October came another newspaper scandal. Gilbert was invited to be one of the guests of honour at a dinner given by local magistrates at an hotel in Hounslow, Middlesex. Because he himself had studied law after leaving Cambridge, he was looking forward to an interesting evening and some entertaining discussion of his sometimes violent views on the anomalies of English law. But, before going to Hounslow, he went to a cocktail party which Noël Coward gave at the Café de Paris. It was for the artists he hoped to persuade to take part in a midnight matinee for charity the following spring. It was an exuberant occasion – and Gilbert's undoing.

The following morning almost every newspaper carried front-page news items with inch-deep headlines: 'Gilbert Harding Ordered Out' . . . 'Gilbert Harding in Dinner Row' . . . 'Harding Calls Magistrates "Third-Rate" '. The story in the *Daily Express* said:

'Gilbert Harding, peppery star of T V and radio, was asked to leave a dinner at the Red Lion Hotel, in Hounslow, last night. He had been driven there as a guest of the local magistrates.

He first startled the guests by lifting up a pheasant from the table and putting it on to a bowl of sprouts carried by a waiter.

When asked to speak he said, "I have been dragged along to this third-rate place for a third-rate dinner for third-rate people".

In the uproar that followed a guest brought Harding's coat and he was taken to the hotel door. He refused to get into the magistrate's Rolls-Royce.

After an argument on the footpath he hailed a taxi and was driven off.

At his Mayfair flat he said later: "It was a horrible, horrible evening. Just another surburban do . . . and I was asked there as Exhibit A." '

Other newspapers stated that, having been dissuaded from continuing his own speech, Gilbert had sat down and, for the next two hours, had made audible comments about the other speakers. They also said that he had insisted on setting off to walk back to London and had only with difficulty been persuaded to get into a taxi.

I quote the newspapers' accounts of the evening because I never knew the truth of the affair. Nor did Gilbert, for he certainly was quite unable to describe to me what had happened.

All the next day we were besieged by reporters – either at the front door or on the telephone. That day the *Evening Standard* reported Gilbert as saying, after reading the reports of his speech the previous evening, 'Oh, did I say that? If I did, you can say that I consider myself fourth-rate. I was very rude last night and behaved abominably. I'm sorry. Every time I behave badly, I am always sorry.' *The Star* reported me as admitting that 'Mr. Harding is ashamed of what he said last night and is very sorry'.

That evening at Hounslow provided the newspapers with material for several weeks. Two nights later Lord Latham – then Lord Lieutenant of Middlesex – was reported as having said to a justices' dinner at Winchmore Hill: 'Many of us were understandably distressed to see it reported that a gorilla was interposed in certain of the televising in the United States of the Coronation of our Queen. But I understand that the manners of the gorilla were exemplary. We must regret that this cannot be said of the performance of a certain television notability at a recent dinner. I notice the person concerned has apologized, as well he should. The only thing in the conduct of this person we can readily accept is his reported statement that he is fourth-rate.'

The press began to publish letters from their readers demanding that in view of his recent behaviour the B B C should sack Gilbert. In the meantime his solicitor and the solicitor for the owner of the Red Lion Hotel were exchanging letters. An action for slander was threatened. Just a week after the dinner, the London newspapers were happy to publish this item:

'We have been asked by Messrs. R. V. Goodhew Ltd., to publish the following letter received by their solicitors from Mr. Gilbert Harding:

"I have already apologized as fully as I can for the unfortunate incidents at the Red Lion Hotel, Hounslow, last Tuesday – for which there is no excuse.

"I am anxious to repair any damage which you might think has been done to your clients, Messrs. R. V. Goodhew Ltd. – for many of whose properties I have a great regard. I did not know until I received your letter that they own the Red Lion Hotel at Hounslow.

"In accordance with the requirements of your letter: (1) I repeat the apology; (2) I confirm that as far as I remember the dinner was very good; (3) As far as I know the Red Lion Hotel at Hounslow is indeed a first-class suburban hotel.

"I do hope that this is the end of the matter." '

Then, a few days later, it was announced that, in consideration of the hotel owners dropping their proposed action, Gilbert had paid one hundred pounds to a charity named by them.

But the matter didn't end there for, under the title *Where Ignorance is Bliss* and with a Norman Mansbridge cartoon showing Gilbert stepping into a railway carriage on which '3rd' had been crossed out and '4th' substituted, *Punch* published an article about his behaviour at Hounslow. In it he was described as 'a leading connoisseur of abuse and ill-manners', 'a man blessed with, to all intents and purposes, a single great gift – that of making himself publicly objectionable for private profit'.

It was a witty, cynical and savage article. Gilbert was very deeply upset by it. He made several angry telephone calls to Malcolm Muggeridge – at that time the editor of *Punch* – and to J. B. Booth-royd, the writer of the article. Once more solicitors got busy and a writ was threatened, this time by Gilbert. But his solicitors advised him against carrying out the threat. They believed that, though he might win, the damages could be humiliatingly small and the resultant publicity would do him further harm.

All in all, that dinner at Hounslow proved to be a chastening and an expensive affair for Gilbert. He later confessed to me that it had been one of the three nightmare occasions of his life. The first had been in Canada, the second when he had walked out on a cricket match in Hertfordshire. He gave me no details, nor did he ever refer to those incidents again. And, as I say, he never gave me any details of the night at Hounslow because, as he confessed, there was a complete blank in his memory from the time he left the Café de Paris to his awakening next morning.

Even while the newspapers were still chewing over that particular scandal, a smaller one came to light. Only two evenings before the magistrates' dinner Gilbert took his friend Mrs. Barbara Back to the first night of *The King and I* at Drury Lane. Most of the gossip columns in the following day's papers reported that he had gone to sleep during the play and had snored loudly. The *Evening Standard* published a letter from someone who had sat near Gilbert in the theatre, complaining of how much the writer, and others sitting near by, had suffered. 'Mr. Harding snored and snored through almost the whole of the first act, making the most disgusting noises in the most objectionable manner. At times we thought he was going to have a fit. My neighbour prodded him, with little success, and it was absolutely impossible to concentrate on the programme.'

Barbara Back told me later that it had been even more impossible for her to concentrate on what, she was convinced, was a magnificent show. Not only had she had to spend most of the time nudging Gilbert, either to try to wake him up or – at the least – to stop his snores, but she had also felt obliged to turn round and shush the shushers. In fact, she had barely caught a glimpse of the stage the whole evening!

As usual, Gilbert apologized handsomely. He sent a telegram to Valerie Hobson, the star of *The King and I*. 'Please don't believe all you read,' it said. 'I only slept when you were not on the stage.' But the telegram was not acknowledged.

I had another reason to remember the opening night of *The King and I*. Gilbert had returned, rather late in the afternoon, from a luncheon appointment which, though obviously lavish, had not left him in a benevolent mood. Yet, while he was changing for the theatre, he suddenly put his hand in his pocket and then thrust a five-pound note towards me. 'That's for you,' he said.

'But what for?' I protested. 'I haven't done anything special, have I? There's nothing to reward me for particularly.'

'No, you're right,' he said. Back went the note into his pocket.

He was ready dressed when Barbara Back arrived, looking quite wonderful in a crimson brocade evening cloak. Gilbert did not stop to admire her. 'This boy has just insulted me by refusing to accept five pounds I wanted to give him,' he grumbled.

'Roger, how could you be so foolish?' asked Barbara. 'Give it to me, Gilbert. I know he won't insult me.'

Gilbert seemed quite content to remain insulted. But Barbara persisted until he handed her the fiver. 'Now, Roger,' said Barbara, 'never refuse money from Gilbert again. He can afford it – and you deserve it. Think of all the people who get money out of him for nothing at all. And think of all you do that you don't get paid for.' I had no hesitation in accepting. Gilbert, whose mood had immediately changed, gave me a sideways gleam and bowed slightly from the waist to Barbara. 'Madam,' he said, 'you are – as always – absolutely right. I can't imagine why Roger hasn't sacked me a dozen times already.'

After that, there were other times when he suddenly insisted on giving me a five-pound note. Once he telephoned to me at Cadogan Place, just as I was about to leave for the evening, to take a girl friend to dinner. He was at his club in Brook Street and asked if I could possibly manage to take him a book he particularly wanted. Since Brook Street was, in any case, on my way, I was at the club, with the book, ten minutes later.

'Ah, Roger, my friend,' was my welcome. 'Come along. You must have a drink and meet some people.'

'It's very kind of you, Mr. Harding,' I said, 'but I'm only just in time to meet a friend I am taking out to dinner. I really mustn't stay.'

'Of course, so you told me earlier, dear boy. Well, have a pleasant evening,' and, as he took the book from my hand, he discreetly replaced it with a note.

When I saw the five pounds in my hand, I realized that, in fact, he had not needed the book at all. He must earlier have wanted to give me something towards the evening's expense and then forgotten. The errand was just a cover for his kindness.

It had already been announced, in September of that year, that *What's My Line?* was to return to the screen on November the first. The date was drawing near and still no announcement of the composition of the panel had been made. Gilbert had caused many minor, and one major scandal since the previous series, so that he began to be very worried indeed that he would not even be asked to appear. He had no confidence at all in himself. 'They don't want me, you know, Roger,' he would say, again and again. 'Why should they indeed? I'm just a phoney anyway – a parlour-game piddler. If I were a tame pussy-cat it might be all right. But I'm not – am I? – even a raging tiger either . . .'

I would try to convince him of my own confidence that the programme would not be at all popular without him.

'Nonsense! Rubbish! Anyone can ask questions – and without getting into hot water too.'

Eventually, only about ten days before the show was to start again, a B B C executive telephoned to ask him to be one of the panel. Gilbert's relief was tremendous and his mood beatific. But it was short-lived. Within twenty-four hours it seemed almost certain that something other than a B B C decision would prevent him from taking his usual part in television's most popular programme.

CHAPTER FOUR

IMPATIENT PATIENT

ONCE more, Gilbert's health let him down. Two days after the telephone call asking him to appear in *What's My Line?* I arrived in the morning to find him quite obviously ill. His face was flushed and he was having great trouble in drawing enough air into his lungs. It was absurd for him to deny it. I telephoned the doctor right away. When he came and examined Gilbert, he found that he had a high temperature and his lungs were again inflamed. Again the order was "a few days' rest". Again I went through the sad and embarrassing task of cancelling engagements. But, on Gilbert's firm instructions, just for four days. 'I'll be well enough for *Twenty Questions* on Monday, Roger. Don't be silly. Of course I will. I've got to be well enough.'

Once more the newspapers announced 'Gilbert Harding Ill – Engagements Cancelled' and, for the next day or two, I was kept busy answering inquiries, holding reporters at bay, arranging arm-fuls of flowers in vases, jam-jars and buckets. By the Saturday after-noon, Gilbert was feeling much better and, since a friend was coming to keep him company for the evening, I was able to leave for home quite early for a change.

At Victoria Station, as I was rushing for my train, his name on a newspaper bill caught my eye. 'Gilbert Harding – Sad News' it announced. I had left him only fifteen minutes earlier but it seemed suddenly that my heart had stopped beating. I thrust coppers into the newsvendor's hand and glanced swiftly at the Stop Press. Nothing. I took a deep breath and everything was normal again. He couldn't, of course, have died and the news been published in fifteen minutes. Then I searched the paper. There, on an inside page, was a short paragraph stating simply that Gilbert Harding was still con-fined to bed and, as previously announced, had been forced to cancel his week-end engagements, though he was making satisfactory progress. But, like me, about ninety per cent of the homeward-bound workers must have been caught. That newsvendor sold out in record time!

It was not the last time that I was to be shocked by a hand-written newspaper bill. Two years later, when Gilbert was in the Brompton Hospital, with what had finally been diagnosed as a rare heart disorder, and was already on the road to recovery, it happened again. I was at the hospital, visiting him, when Sister called me to the telephone. It was Kate Wadleigh, calling from *The People*. The day before, she had seen Gilbert and discussed the column with him as he sat, in his dressing-gown, on a hard, straight chair beside the bed – 'I'm not ill enough to be in bed *all* the time. Besides, I can't breathe lying down.' Now it was Friday; the column was being printed. 'But someone just telephoned me to say he had seen a poster saying, "Gilbert Harding – Sinking". Is it true, Roger?' I was able to say, with complete authority, that it wasn't. He was not only sitting up on that hard chair, but demanding that he should now be allowed to go home again.

But, naturally, within the next few hours, the telephone rang continuously. Friends, who knew where he was, deluged the hospital with inquiries. Newspaper reporters scurried around, sent telegrams and telephone messages. The rumour had spread like a forest fire.

Eventually, we traced its source. A newspaper-seller in Oxford Street anxious to avoid a damp, cold evening, had devised his own poster. And the speed with which he had disposed of the newspapers had enabled him to get away home long before anyone could catch up with him to correct it.

Obviously, everyone enjoys tragic news, particularly the press. Years later, when Gilbert was in University College Hospital, he was very close to death. Then, almost miraculously, he began to improve and, within three weeks, had nearly recovered. One evening, when the doctors were considering allowing him to come home, Joan Smith – his Brighton housekeeper – and I had visited him and then, to celebrate his recovery, gone to the cinema. When we got back to the flat, the telephone was ringing as I opened the door. It was the *Daily Mail* calling. 'Is is true that Mr. Harding has taken a turn for the worse and is on the danger list again?' The reporter said that they had received this information from three different sources during the last hour. I told him, curtly, that his informants were entirely mistaken: 'Mr. Harding's improvement is maintained.'

Almost immediately the phone rang again. It was 'Midge', the daily help at Brighton who, in Joan's absence, was sleeping in the house. She said the newspapers had telephoned her twice to ask if it was true that Gilbert had had a relapse. She was very deeply distressed and it was some time before we could sufficiently calm her down to accept our assurance that it was yet another false alarm. But, when we had done so, Joan and I both realized that we ourselves had become more than a little disturbed. 'All right,' I said, 'I'll ring Sister. It won't do any harm.' We were both left with rather shamefaced grins when the night sister reported that she had looked in on Gilbert only five minutes before and found him sleeping peacefully, his breathing and his pulse steadier than they had been for several days.

But other newspapers had picked up this baseless rumour. The telephone began to ring again, as each one of the dailies called for confirmation or denial. By two o'clock, we decided that the rumour must have been killed, so I went home and to bed. When I arrived back at nine the following morning, Joan had already been awake for three busy hours denying the rumour of a relapse all over again!

This may sound as though we were constantly at war with newspaper reporters. We were not. However irritating it was to answer the same question seven or eight times an hour, I could always easily convince myself that 'they are only doing the job they have been given to do'. That was exactly what I was doing myself. Often it was sympathy for the harassed reporters that kept me at the telephone long after I might have escaped into silence in my own flat. So it was delightful – and rather moving – to receive quite a different kind of press call soon after that occasion when Gilbert was apparently dying at U C H. It came from a Fleet Street public-house. The speaker said that he had been asked by a group of reporters there present, representing nearly every national newspaper group and news agency, to thank us for our pleasant and helpful attitude towards the press throughout Gilbert's illness.

But all that lay a long way ahead. On that occasion at Cadogan Place, the newsvendor had grossly exaggerated. The news continued to be 'progressing satisfactorily' and, on the Monday, though he was still far from well, Gilbert insisted on appearing on *Twenty Questions*. In those days, before a succession of serious illnesses had sadly weakened his resistance, his powers of recovery constantly amazed me. Often I would arrive at the flat in the morning to find him quite obviously unwell, and with a full day's engagements

c*

ahead of him. Time and again I was sure he would not be able to go
through with them. Time and again he showed me how wrong I was.

I am not speaking of hangovers. Gilbert never had one. 'Perhaps if
I woke up feeling like death, I wouldn't drink so much,' he often
said. 'But I don't. I don't have a bad head or stomach upsets or the
shakes. There must be something wrong with me.' It was true. Very
often, after a heavy night's drinking in those days, he was up before
eight o'clock, well and cheerful and ready for the day's work. 'Not
feeling well', then, almost always meant that he had difficulty in
breathing.

That was the case when, against the doctor's wishes, Gilbert went
to the *Twenty Questions* studio that night. I went with him and,
long before the broadcast was over, I could clearly see that he was
feeling very much worse. But he didn't sound so. His public personality was in control. From the studio he went straight home to bed
and the doctor, when he called the next morning, insisted that his
rest should continue. For the fourth time in two months he was
ordered to bed. For the fourth time I had to cancel his engagements.
For the fourth time the newspaper headlines recorded the stages of
his illness in their headlines.

The first programme of the new *What's My Line?* series was only
six days ahead and Gilbert was frantically anxious to be allowed to
take his place on the panel. The doctor thought that, provided he
really did relax completely, he might be well enough by then. So,
taking the risk, we told the B B C and the reporters that he would
definitely be taking part in the programme. But the days that
followed were very trying for Gilbert. He was frightened by the
breakdown of his health; he was afraid that he might not be well
enough in time for *What's My Line?* and he was sincerely upset to
have disappointed people by having to 'give back word' – a
northern phrase both he and I understood, meaning to break a
promise. Two of the cancelled engagements had been for charity –
one of them a brains trust on behalf of a fund for spastic children
and the other a Roman Catholic church bazaar at Ilford. He bitterly
regretted not being able to keep his promise to help. His nerves were
taut. His temper suffered – and so did those who were trying to help
him and to nurse him.

He was allowed to have very few visitors, and those only two or
three close friends or business colleagues. So he quickly grew tired of
the faces he saw so regularly – Mrs. Clarke's and mine. We got on
his nerves – and he said so. 'For heaven's sake, go away and leave

me in peace. I can't stand either of you creeping around the place as if I were dying. Go away. Go away – and don't come back!' But, if he were left alone for five minutes, it was, 'Roger! Roger! Where are you? What are you doing? What's going on? Whatever do you think I pay the two of you for . . . to sit around idly gossiping, while I lie here sick and helpless?'

Another kind of crisis came in the middle of that week. For some time before his illness the proofs of his life story for *John Bull* had been arriving for revision and correction. He had continually put off attending to them until a telephone call came from the editor of the magazine, to say that the proofs must be corrected and returned to their office by the end of the week if they were to be published on the date already announced. The book, too, was almost ready for publication. It was to come out after the first two or three instalments had appeared in *John Bull*. In order to save time, Odham's Press and Putnam's (the book's publishers) had agreed that one set of corrected proofs would do for both. From our point of view, this made added confusion, for the projected instalments for *John Bull* did not necessarily coincide with the beginning and end of the book's chapters. So, for weeks, they had not been touched.

Now, with Gilbert at a loose end, seemed to be the moment to bring them to his notice and to keep him occupied. 'This is a splendid opportunity to get on with the proofs,' I suggested brightly and laid them before him. He agreed and we started. It wasn't long before he began to get irritated by the seeming clashes between magazine and book version. The bed became strewn with long, writhing galley proofs. Finally, with one great heave, he threw the lot from him. 'Telephone the publishers! Get on to *John Bull*! Get hold of those numbskulls and tell them to come here and sort out their own snakes' nest!' he howled.

Having had a little experience of publishing in my previous job, I understood the inconsistencies that puzzled him and I tried, calmly, to explain them. Perhaps I am at my most irritating when I am right, when I know I am right and am trying to persuade some-one else to believe it. I certainly irritated Gilbert that day. Soon petulance gave place to anger, anger to fury and fury to a near fit.

'Get out of my sight, you knowledgeable prig! You pettifogging publisher's-assistant-secretary! Don't dare to tell *me* how to read proofs. Do you think I'm an illiterate ignoramus? Get out, before I . . .'

I was only too glad to escape his torrential wrath, but I had only just closed the bedroom door behind me when I heard a series of shattering explosions from his room. I blandly assured myself that as long as he was capable of such activity, he needed no ministrations of mine. So I went into the next room and sat down long enough to relax a little. When I went back into the bedroom, drawing a long, steadying breath as I did so, I was just in time to see the contents of the last of a considerable number of medicine bottles from his bedside table trickling slowly down the splintered remnants of his dressing-table mirror. His medicines had not come from the National Health Service and their replacement, together with the cost of the landlord's broken mirror, added a bit to the expense of his illness. But no word was said about his outburst. We got the proofs corrected, quite quietly and soberly, in the next two days.

On the day of that eruption, however, a friend – the mother of a growing boy – called to see Gilbert. During their conversation she told him that the next day she was taking her son to be fitted for his first long trousers. 'Where are you having them made?' he asked her. When she told him, he turned to me. 'Write that down, would you, Roger?' he said. Then he turned back to the mother. 'Please,' he said, 'would you allow me to make this a gift from me? No, listen. I remember so well my own first pair of long trousers. Ma and I were in X——s, the best tailor in Hereford, ordering them, when one of the "gentry" came in. He was a dear old man who had known us for a long time. A week later, when we went to collect the parcel, the tailor told us the old gentleman had paid for them and asked us to accept it as a token of his appreciation of the importance of the occasion. Ma, who had planned sacrifices to go to this tailor – she always believed that the best is cheapest in the end – was delighted. So was I. When we got home, I tried them on at once. I swaggered about, put my hands in the pockets – and found something in each of them. A bright half-sovereign.'

The next day, I telephoned the tailor and passed on Gilbert's instructions. The bill was to be sent to him, with the addition of twenty shillings. I had to instruct him that, when he delivered the suit, each trouser pocket must contain a brand new ten-shilling note. 'I only wish,' said Gilbert wistfully, 'that I could discover a couple of golden half-sovereigns somewhere.'

Many reporters and journalists sought bedside interviews with Gilbert that week, but they all had to be refused. One of the most persistent was Miss Nancy Baume, of *Reveille*. She first telephoned to ask for an interview. I explained that the doctor had ordered absolute rest and no visitors. A few hours later, Miss Baume announced herself at the front door and made the same request. Again the answer was no. Only an hour later she returned, with an armful of flowers, and asked me to 'give Mr. Harding the best wishes' of her editor. 'Thank you,' I said. 'Please tell your editor how much Mr. Harding appreciates his kindness. But you still can't interview him.' She gave a creditable performance of one who had never for a moment supposed otherwise. Ninety minutes later she was back again, carrying a parcel of books, and looking as though she only just managed to hold her tears in check. She thrust the books at me and explained, in a rush of words, that naturally this kind of thing wasn't natural to her. It went against the grain, of course. But her editor – who could be very difficult – absolutely insisted that she get some kind of story about Mr. Harding. Please, could I help her? Could I say how he passed his time? Did he read – and if so, what sort of books? Did he wear pyjamas – or a nightshirt? What kind of medicine was he taking? What did he eat . . . drink . . . talk about? What were his fans saying and writing? Of course, she wouldn't dream of suggesting in anything she wrote that she had actually seen Mr. Harding himself. But she could do some sort of piece about him, if I would just be terribly kind and help her a little.

By this time I was not only a bit weary of the questioning; I was also a trifle worried on Miss Baume's account. I began to wonder whether the flowers and the books would, in fact, be recouped on her expense account. I had a painful feeling that they were a personal, desperate last throw. So I gave her the answer to most of her questions. But she appeared to be in no hurry to get away and write them down. 'What a very interesting job you must have,' she said. 'Have you been very long with Mr. Harding?' She said I seemed very young for such a responsible post. 'Have you always been a secretary?' It developed into quite a cosy chat. The apparent object of her importunity seemed to be asleep. He didn't call. We just stood in the hall talking, I thought, aimlessly. Then I took Miss Baume to the front door, said good night and forgot her and *Reveille*.

A few days later – it was a Saturday – I realized that more than one person had used the words 'shock-absorber' when speaking to me. I must admit that I thought it apt, but it seemed strange that others, simultaneously, had reached the same conclusion. It was only when one of the local shopkeepers greeted me slyly with 'And how is the shock-absorber today?' that I realized here was something more than coincidence I asked what he meant. He seemed surprised that I didn't know .'Didn't you see *Reveille*?' I said I hadn't, and raced to the nearest newsagent to buy it. On an inside page there was a headline, nearly two inches deep, 'Shock-Absorber to Human Volcano.'

'Roger Storey has a job that would make many a seasoned diplomat shiver and turn pale.' Miss Baume's article began. 'He is thirty-one and his work calls for an almost superhuman quota of tact. He is private secretary to the nation's most explosive personality – Gilbert Harding.' Miss Baume's memory was bad – I had told her I was twenty-seven – but her imagination was lively enough, for there followed a highly coloured, if somewhat inaccurate, account of my employer in the role of an invalid.

She did, of course, get near the truth on one or two points, particularly when she wrote, 'For every two or three of the volcanic Harding outbursts that hit the public in the solar plexus at such regular intervals, there must be many similar near-episodes that are hushed, dissolved, dispersed and lulled out of existence by this perfect secretary who has to act as a buffer so often.' Miss Baume, obviously drawing on the recollection of her earlier visits, described how we had been deep in conversation when 'there was a sort of muffled roar from the bedroom, like deep thunder, and the secretary jumped as though he had been stung'. She told how Mrs. Clarke appeared and said 'in ominous tones, *"Mr. Harding wants you."* Britain's number one buffer squared his slim shoulders, gave me a debonair wave as I departed and made for the bedroom door.'

I was at first horrified. Then, as I read on, I found myself becoming flattered that any paper should think me of such interest that they would waste half a page on me. I was grinning with delight until I realized that someone was bound to tell Gilbert about it and that he might think I had been deliberately showing off. I decided I must tell him about it before anyone else did, so I took the paper to the office with me. 'Just look at this nonsense,' I said, handing it to him. I shook slightly while he read it through to the end without comment. Finally, he looked up with a wry smile. 'I don't know what you're fussing about,' he said. 'When you've been misquoted and misrepresented as often as I have, you'll learn to take no notice at all of this kind of thing. And don't imagine it's the last time, either. Now the newspapers have got hold of your name, they'll ascribe all sorts of strange sayings to you. You'll just have to get used to it.'

In the next few weeks *London Opinion, Television News* and *Men Only* all published articles about Gilbert in which there were several references to me, though this time I was not quoted. But, after the first shock of *Reveille*, I ceased to worry. I rather enjoyed 'seeing my name in the papers'.

It was not the only kind of reflected glory I got from working for Gilbert Harding. It was flattering, when I went on my own to some of the very smart shops he dealt at, to be recognized and treated as courteously and efficiently as he would have been. When, with friends, I visited restaurants to which he had previously taken me, it was amusing – and, of course, very impressive – to be greeted by the head waiter, led to one of the best tables and have two or three waiters hovering around, anticipating every need. I sometimes contemplated a Stephen Potter-ish article on 'How to be treated like a celebrity, without actually being one.' Occasionally, I was even able to get theatre seats at short notice, in spite of Sold Out notices, just by mentioning that I was Gilbert Harding's secretary.

Naturally it worked the other way as well. Some shop assistants deliberately refused to see me waiting at the counter. Others sniffed audibly when they were asked to charge items to Mr. Harding's account. In one or two restaurants the waiters did all they could to avoid coming anywhere near my table. They obviously expected me to demand the impeccable service Gilbert required.

Once I was refused the tenancy of a flat when the landlord's agent found out that I was Gilbert's secretary. He explained that 'noisy parties would upset the other tenants and would not be in keeping with the amenities of our property'. In vain I protested that I had not the time, the inclination or the money to hold parties – noisy or quiet. The agent was adamant. That was certainly a true reflection from my employer, for the same thing happened to him some years later. He was about to sign the lease of a flat in Kensington Gore when the landlord discovered that his would-be tenant was *the* Gilbert Harding. The landlord stopped the negotiations. He had 'had that type of person before'. He wasn't going to have noisy parties going on all night on his property. He knew what those B B C types were.

My job gave me a social standing which, with my normal provincial middle-class background and lack of attainments, I had never known before. I became an object of interest and a centre of attention whenever anyone found out about my job. I never announced it, because I soon learned that it always met with one or two equally awkward responses. One type of person always gasped and said, 'How marvellous! What a wonderful job! What a fascinating life you must have!' They implied that I must live in luxury and at leisure off the fat of the land. They thought Gilbert was 'terrific and they knew that his outbursts of bad temper were only 'put on for effect'. To them I just murmured agreement, but I found it difficult not to say, 'You just try it, that's all! If you think his bad temper is phoney, then he's a greater actor than Gielgud, Olivier, Orson Welles and the lot.'

The other reaction came from those who disliked Gilbert. They thought he was the most ill-tempered, bad-mannered, useless and nasty man they had ever seen or heard. The unemployment figures might be high, they said, but surely even I could find something less humiliating than my present job. Had I no pride? To them I found no difficulty at all in singing Gilbert's praises. I maintained, with warmth, that I had found him kind, thoughtful, considerate and entertaining. 'Of course he has a bad temper, but it quickly blows over and he never harbours a grudge. He never says one thing to your face and another behind your back.' As those who disliked him were mainly people who had never met him or, if they had, then just once in unhappy circumstances, it was not hard to convince them that I knew him better than they and spoke with authority.

Of course my close friends knew that I worked for Gilbert, but many of my acquaintances had no idea how I was employed. When I was asked, I usually said that I worked for a man who wrote and occasionally broadcast on specialized subjects. I hoped that would sound dreary enough not to warrant further explanation. I got so tired of the discussions that inevitably followed once Gilbert's name was mentioned. Besides, like most people, I liked to leave my job behind me in the office. The ruse almost always worked. People rarely pressed me to explain the 'specialized subjects'. This may sound pretentiously elaborate, but it became very important to me, for I realized that I could easily get lost in the shadow of a celebrity. The possibility struck me very forcibly when, one day, a woman I had known all my life introduced me to a friend of hers by saying simply 'and this is Gilbert Harding's secretary'.

When Gilbert was in good health and fulfilling all his engagements, my public importance naturally dwindled. On that occasion, after his six days' rest, he realized his wish and was fit enough for the first programme of the *What's My Line?* series. That was the time when Lady Barnett first joined the panel, and, before she did so, Gilbert privately frowned on the idea. He felt that the old team had worked really well together and that a new member would slow the programme down – particularly as Lady Barnett ('And she needn't think I'm going to call her by her Christian name,' said Gilbert) was a newcomer to television and a complete amateur. I began to be afraid that this prejudice would turn his occasional exasperation with the programme into a permanent grudge.

So the morning after the first appearance, I asked him with some temerity what he thought of the newcomer. Without any reservation at all, he said she was absolutely delightful. As far as the viewers and critics were concerned, it took Lady Barnett several weeks to settle down in *What's My Line?* Some people thought she was very dull and demanded that she be replaced. 'Over my dead body,' was Gilbert's reaction to this suggestion, as he continued to defend her inclusion on the panel. Everyone who knows a celebrity is asked, 'What is so-and-so really like?' Whenever Gilbert was asked this question about Lady Barnett, he replied. 'Isobel is one of the very few people I know who are just as pleasant and charming as they appear to be.'

I was able to agree with him wholeheartedly when I met her at a cocktail party given by Gilbert. She was, indeed, charming – to me, as to everybody else. I have since met her many times, though at long intervals; yet she has never failed to recognize me and to remember my name. Considering how many people she must meet, privately and officially, this kindliness always surprises and delights me. The same thing is true of Eamonn Andrews and Kenneth Horne. But, apart from this entirely selfish reason for liking them, they seem to be three of the most genuinely friendly and likeable celebrities I have ever met.

That cocktail party of Gilbert's started out as a plan for just a small affair – 'not more than thirty to thirty-five people' – but it ended with at least a hundred guests. Fortunately, from the beginning he had not intended to hold it in his gloomy flat but had booked a private room at a Piccadilly restaurant. The idea was partly to return hospitality to many friends, but mainly in honour of Bill and Ella Gladstone-Murry, old friends from his days as a representative of the BBC in Canada. Mr. Gladstone-Murry had been one of the small handful of people working at Savoy Hill in the days when British radio was 2LO. He it was who had first thought of publishing the *Radio Times* and he had had the satisfaction of seeing it become one of the greatest publishing successes of the age.

Because both the host and the guest of honour were closely concerned with broadcasting, the B B C was well represented at the party by past and present executives. I was a little overawed to meet so many V I Ps for the first time and all at once. These B B C executives had spasmodically worried me for days. I had learned by heart the names of all the guests invited to the party: many of the names I knew, of course, but I had met no more than half a dozen. Some I would be sure to recognize on sight, but others would be quite unidentifiable. I need not have worried. One of the first things I had noticed, and appreciated about Gilbert was the meticulous way in which he introduced me to people. Whoever it was I was meeting – distinguished members of his club or the driver of a hired car – I was introduced to them properly by name. Because of this I was always made to feel a part of the conversation, however casual, rather than someone who just happened to be around.

On this occasion he introduced me to Bernard Braden and Barbara Kelly, to Frances Day and Elizabeth Allan. Gilbert had known the Bradens in Canada and Barbara was one of the regulars on *What's My Line?* They were gay and friendly guests. Vivacious Frances Day had been one of my idols for years – ever since I had heard her sing *It's delightful, it's delicious, it's delovely* on the radio; and I thought Elizabeth Allan one of the loveliest women I had ever seen. I met Frances Day only once afterwards, but, happily, I saw the Bradens and Miss Allan and her husband, Bill O'Bryen, on many occasions.

But I did have one slightly embarrassing moment. I had felt fairly certain of recognizing the late Sir George, and Lady Barnes (he was then Director of Television) for I had met them, briefly, a few weeks earlier. 'Ah, there's Lady Barnes,' I said to myself and, as she was standing alone, I went across to speak to her. I mentioned that I knew very few people there and felt rather shy. She said she was in pretty much the same position. 'At the moment,' she said, 'the only person I can recognize is Leonard Russell.' I expressed admiration for Mr. Russell, the Literary Editor of the *Sunday Times* and said we had often spoken on the telephone but never met. 'Well, then, I shall introduce you,' said the lady. 'He's my husband.' I suddenly realized I had been talking, not to Lady Barnes, but to Dilys Powell, whose film criticisms had delighted and guided me for many years.

I muttered an apology and prayed that the floor might open. But her reply to my apology won my heart and my gratitude. 'Anne Barnes and I were at school together and there's no one I'd rather be mistaken for.'

At another of Gilbert's parties, there was a much more widely assorted list of guests. The party was organized and paid for by Hulton's, for Gilbert was by then writing a weekly column about television for their *Picture Post,* and photographs of the party were to illustrate his Christmas feature in the magazine. Here there were not only B B C personalities, producers, staff and technicians, but even some of the previous challengers on *What's My Line?* whom he had been said to have insulted. There were many of these to invite: some politely declined, a few impolitely refused, others ignored the invitation. Only a handful turned up, among them Philip Paul, the ghost-hunter of whom Gilbert had said, 'You must be barmy.' He turned out to be a most likeable man. After the host had renewed his apologies, they became very friendly. Among the B B C personalities who came were Ronnie Waldman, at that time Head of Television Light Entertainment, with his film star wife, Lana Morris; Frankie Howerd; Norman Wisdom and the lovely Lady Boyle. At that time Catherine Boyle had made only a few appearances on television, in *Quite Contrary,* where all that was required of her was to be beautiful and silent. Gilbert had openly wondered if she *could* speak. At the party he discovered she could, with charm and vivacity.

But parties did his health no good and, on his doctor's advice, Gilbert consulted a specialist in diseases of the chest. It was decided that he was suffering from some form of asthma and bronchitis and, unless he had early treatment, it would get very much worse in the near future. Obviously, he was very much overweight and this contributed to his more frequently recurring difficulty in breathing. The doctors wanted him to go into a nursing home for a few weeks. There he would have to follow a strict diet, to give up smoking and drinking and to take a course of drugs, all of which might achieve a complete cure. Gilbert was horrified. He so impressed the doctors with his horror of hospitals and nursing homes that eventually they agreed to allow him to have the treatment at home. They insisted that, though he could fulfil his radio and television engagements, all other commitments must be cancelled and he must spend as much time as possible in bed. How soon could the regimen begin?

It was a difficult decision for Gilbert. It was nearing the last week in November and in his diary there was not a single day before January on which there was no entry. One particular day in mid-December was a very important one for him. He was to be the guest of honour at Foyle's Literary Luncheon to mark the publication of his autobiography, *Along My Line*. That same evening he was to act as chairman of a brains trust at Hammersmith Hospital – a light-hearted affair, but with distinguished surgeons and physicians on the panel. Gilbert had promised Matron, weeks before, that he would be there and he was looking forward to it. He told the doctors he would put himself in their hands on the following day. Very reluctantly, they agreed.

Immediately, of course, the B B C had to be forewarned and they offered to deal with newspaper inquiries, so that they could make it perfectly clear that he would continue his radio and television appearances. But the engagements he could not keep had to be cancelled at once. The news began to leak out. Soon the telephone line to Cadogan Place was choked with inquiries. It was a relief to be able to refer reporters to the B B C press officer, but naturally Gilbert's friends had to be given fuller details of his condition. Still, we did not avoid confusion. Newspaper columnists telephoned to ask how many *What's My Line?* programmes Mr. Harding was expected to miss. What about *Twenty Questions?* Would he still write his columns for *Picture Post* and *The People?* Over and over again, dozens of times a day, I had to repeat that he would fulfil all his B B C and journalistic commitments but that everything else was cancelled.

As the day – a Thursday – drew near when the new regimen would begin, we discussed how to make it as pleasant as possible. Because the bedroom at the back of the flat was so grimly gloomy, we decided to move his bed into the sitting-room. But this involved much more than just carting a piece of furniture from one room to another. Gilbert left for Newquay early on the Monday morning, to return on Tuesday afternoon. Mrs. Clarke and I, electricians and Post Office engineers, went to work.

Bells were to be installed in the dining-room – my office – and in Mrs. Clarke's flat below, so that there would never be a moment when Gilbert could not summon one of us. The radiogram had to be moved to make room for the bed, and yet be near enough for him to operate as he lay there. The television set had to be similarly re-fixed. The extension telephone in the sitting-room had to be silenced and yet left so that it could be used – though not by the patient in bed.

When we had got the bed into position, we realized that it took up much more room than we had supposed. The sitting-room was overcrowded with furniture. Eventually, we pushed, heaved and shoved several pieces out of the room, along the angled corridor and into the bedroom. And, all the time, the telephone rang, letters of urgent inquiry flowed through the letter-box, and all had to be answered.

By the time Gilbert returned on Tuesday afternoon – rather quarrelsome from having travelled in the buffet car – I was utterly exhausted. My back ached, my throat was sore, I had a thundering headache and a running nose. But only three or four jobs remained to be done. One of them was to cancel the place which he had reserved at his club's annual Christmas dinner, about ten days ahead. Several times I had attempted to do so, but the secretary's number had always been engaged. So, naturally, the first question Gilbert asked was, 'Have you cancelled that Christmas dinner?' I explained why I hadn't. And all hell broke loose. 'I suppose you thought that didn't matter. It never occurred to you, did it, that every single member of the club wants a ticket and dozens of them can't get in? You wouldn't care, of course, if there was an empty seat in the name of Gilbert Harding and everyone thought I was too selfish to remember someone else wanted it. What, in the name of Beelzebub, have you been doing since I left?'

I looked dazedly round the sitting-room. 'All right,' I said. 'That's one thing I haven't been able to do. Why don't you ask me about some of the things I *have* done?' Gilbert was astonished. 'Why should I give a twopenny damn about the things you have done?' he thundered. 'It's what you haven't done that's important.' I could stand it no longer. I pointed out that Mrs. Clarke and I had worked very hard and very long to ensure his comfort. I told him how every job I had started had been interrupted again and again by the telephone and by urgent letters. 'All right,' I finished, 'I know you're not well. Neither am I. I feel like death. But you've got weeks of rest ahead of you. I haven't. All I can look forward to is coping with your troubles.'

After that he was silent. I thought I had shamed him into silence and felt a little ashamed myself. But I was mistaken. It was, apparently, the shock of realizing that anyone could be so unfeeling as to speak in such terms to a sick man which had silenced him. For weeks afterwards he retold the story, in his version, to anyone who would listen. 'Did I ever tell you what Roger said to me the day before I was ill?' he asked his doctor one day. 'Yes, Gilbert – at least six times,' was the answer. 'But it's a little different each time, so do tell me again. Those who must care for a strong personality like you have to find some weapon to defend themselves. It seems that Roger has found his. It's no use trying to turn the same weapon against him. In your hands it is blunt.' Gilbert never mentioned the incident again.

On the last, busy day of his freedom, he woke in a splendid mood, declaring that he had not felt so well for weeks. He was a little nervous of the Literary Luncheon, but not of the brains trust. 'I am absolutely determined to enjoy myself today,' he announced, dramatically. 'Tomorrow and tomorrow and tomorrow, leads on . . . to pills and potions and paucity.' He began to dress for lunch. 'Are you ready, Roger?' he asked. 'But I'm not going,' I said. 'Why ever not?' barked Gilbert, as though I were insulting him. 'Because I wasn't invited.' For a moment, he didn't believe me; then he was genuinely horrified.

Originally, Foyle's had asked him to nominate between fifteen and twenty guests of his own choosing – apart from the already agreed guests of honour. Together we had worked on the list, rejecting and selecting. Finally, twenty names were submitted to Foyle's. Though I had no particular wish to be included in the list, the very fact that Gilbert had not suggested putting me on it, had a little hurt me. Now I realized that he had taken it for granted that I would be there. He was quite disproportionately upset and wanted to telephone at once to Christina Foyle and to the Dorchester to put things right – pointing out, very realistically, that at this late stage it would not be possible to choose where I should sit.

I begged him not to do so. I really had no great desire to attend the lunch and, anyway, as I demonstrated, I had come to work – as I usually did – in an elderly suit and would feel very uncomfortable at a fashionable luncheon party. Reluctantly, Gilbert gave in and went off in a taxi by himself.

The occasion was a great success. Lady Astor presided; Lord Boothby (then Sir Robert) proposed the health of Gilbert Harding; the guests of honour included Elizabeth Allan, Aneurin Bevan, the Duchess of Marlborough, Eamonn Andrews, Mrs. Bessie Braddock, M.P., and Philip Harben. Lady Astor began by saying that she had never found herself in stranger company – 'The Mau-Mau would be a rest cure after this.' It seemed that she had been pressed from both sides – by Gilbert and Sir Robert – to say that she was sitting next to 'the most handsome and best-loved men in England today'. They were also, of course, both staunch drinkers. 'If I thought that drink made happier homes, I would support it,' said Lady Astor, 'but when I look around me, I become convinced that I am going to remain sober to my dying day.'

Sir Robert remained unruffled. Of Lady Astor, he said: 'We know that her bark is much worse than her bite. In our heart of hearts we rather enjoy her bark.' And of Gilbert: 'He may not always be his own sweet self, but at least he's always himself.' Of the guests of honour: 'All are handsome, all are distinguished, all are plump – and not one abstains. This should give Lady Astor food for thought.'

Then Gilbert spoke. 'I find myself at a disadvantage. Not only have Sir Robert and I had a very difficult time in drinking an amount of gin equal to Lady Astor's orangeade, but we have also been constantly admonished as to how we should behave. I must keep my foot from faltering, my tongue from chattering, my speech from slipping. And I have to stop being plump – that is something to which I propose to devote attention for the next few weeks.' He finished his speech by telling the assembled company, 'I am glad to have been asked here, and if you have read my book, I think it serves you right.'

Quite clearly, Lady Astor's admonishments had had no effect on Gilbert. When he returned to Cadogan Place he made straight for bed. There he stayed until I woke him about half an hour before the arrival of the car which was to take him to Hammersmith. As he left, he was again quite sober. This sobriety lasted, apparently, only until the brains trust was behind him.

When I arrived next morning I found him desperately struggling for breath. His face was ashen. Haltingly, and with many pauses to fight for air, he told me how he had intentionally got very, very drunk, come home in the early hours and fallen into bed. Then, not much later, waking with a great thirst, he had got up to get a drink from the kitchen tap. Forgetting he was not in his usual bedroom, he had floundered in the dark and fallen heavily over a small coffee table. Badly shaken, and with bruised and aching ribs, he had crawled back to bed to wait, without help or comfort, until my arrival.

Although the doctor and specialist were both expected at eleven o'clock, I knew I must try to get them earlier. Both had already left to visit other patients. The specialist's secretary said she would try to get into touch with his assistant and ask him to call on Gilbert at once. Luckily, Kate Wadleigh was due to call that morning. She was to get two *People* columns – one dealing with his illness, one for the Christmas issue. She was bringing a photographer to take a picture of Gilbert in bed for the head of the column.

When they arrived, Gilbert was very slowly pacing the room. He tried to get back into bed for the photograph but, clearly, it was beyond his powers. Kate and I were of one mind: the photographer was dismissed right away. So the three of us waited for the doctor. We persuaded Gilbert to sit down. Wrapped in an eiderdown, clutching a hot-water bottle, immediately beside the electric fire, he sat in an upright chair, trembling. He was very frightened. So were we, but we assured him again and again, in response to his anxious suppositions, that he would not have to go into hospital.

To take his mind off himself, Kate said: 'We've got a Christmas column to do, Gilbert. Tell me about the Christmases you had when you were a small boy.' Holding tightly to her hand, clutching his hot-water bottle, he began to whisper . . . 'We didn't ever have our own Christmas Day on the twenty-fifth. That was *really* Christmas Day in the workhouse. Ma had worked so hard to make it a rich, happy day for the old, poor people. We had to wait . . . We took round the sweets and joined in the carols . . .' Many days later, when I read Gilbert's Christmas column in *The People*, knowing how the hearts of his readers would expand to his warmth, I wondered how they would have looked on that strangly moving experience. The great popular figure, ill and afraid, leaning on the affection – not of friends or relatives – but of two secretaries through whom he worked, and losing his fears in faraway memories.

The specialist's assistant arrived. Slowly, painfully, we got Gilbert into bed so that he could be examined. The doctor confirmed what we had suspected. He feared that several ribs were broken and that this had further damaged the already weakened lungs. But he dare not give a sedative until a more thorough examination could be made by the specialist.

He had to leave then. Kate had to get back to the office, too. I was left alone to support Gilbert – now out of bed again and standing by the electric fire, quivering with fear and shock. He seemed absolutely unconscious of the heat, while I, unable to retreat, slowly grilled, until I could have sworn I smelled burning flesh. Suddenly, relief came. The room filled with doctors. The three of them probed, prodded and questioned, while Gilbert assured them that he was feeling very much better and there really wasn't much wrong with him. They were not so reassuring. Without x-rays, they said, it was not possible to decide how serious the damage, if any, was. They urged him to go – if only for one night – to hospital so that this could be ascertained. Gilbert protested. The doctors retired to consult together. The moment the door closed, Gilbert tried to make me promise to frustrate any attempt to take him to hospital. After a few moments the assistant returned and said he would stay with Mr. Harding while the other doctors had a word with me. I felt absolutely unreal. It seemed ridiculous that I should be called into conference, in this solemn way, by important medical consultants. Nevertheless, I joined them in the dining-room. It was obvious, they told me, that shock, on top of the original illness, had brought on pneumonia. It was imperative that Gilbert should be moved to a hospital.

So, in face of the persuasions of the four of us, Gilbert had to give in. After innumerable telephone calls, the specialist announced that an ambulance would take the patient to the London Clinic that evening. He gave Gilbert a morphia injection which, he told me, would ease the pain and lull Gilbert to sleep. They would be back, he hoped, before he woke. If not, he was on no account to be allowed to get out of bed: that would almost certainly lead to another fall, with dire results. As I showed them to the door, it was apparent that Gilbert was already asleep.

I stood talking at the front door for a moment or two, as the doctor gave me instructions. I saw him to his car and shut the door. Now, it seemed, my ignorant, if willing, responsibility was over. I drew a deep breath of relief. Then I went back to the sick-room. The patient was no longer asleep. In his dressing-gown, on the far side of the room, he was picking up the telephone. As I came in, he took his hand from the receiver.

'All right, Podge,' he said, in a completely controlled voice, 'let's face it. No one ever went to hospital for one night. Once they get me in there, they aren't going to let me go so easily. I've got to warn the B B C of what's happening.' He picked up the telephone again, spoke to the executive in charge of his programmes and then to the Press Office. Between them, they arranged the announcement to be made to the newspapers and Gilbert specifically asked that it should include a request that no inquiries should be directed to Cadogan Place.

That made two things clear. It was not the first time Gilbert had called me Podge – but, because this time the nickname implied nothing but affectionate co-operation, it took its place as a milestone of my position and I accepted it without resentment. Secondly, there was apparent for the first time his quite remarkable resistance to drugs. I had blandly accepted the doctor's confident assurance that Gilbert would sleep for hours. Yet here he was, clear-headed and calm, dealing in a businesslike way with the essential public aspects of his illness.

This resistance to drugs was later to prove a puzzle to his doctors. After making his telephone calls, despite my appeals to him to get back into bed, Gilbert turned his attention to preparing a list of the things he would need to take to hospital with him. He paced the room, dictating item after item, until I began to fear I would have to pack a couple of cabin trunks. Every few minutes, he had to stop as the coughing shook him painfully. At last, as one severe bout passed, I interrupted.

'Mr. Harding, the ambulance is due in about four hours. If I am to find and pack all the things already on this list, I shall barely have time before it arrives. If you went back to bed now, I could make a start.'

I think he was relieved at the excuse. I helped him to bed and within a few minutes he was asleep, though uneasily. Now Mrs. Clarke had returned home from her job in the City, so she was able to sit with him while I ran backwards and forwards on tiptoe, collecting things and piling them up, rather like a hamster. Apart from the obvious things like pyjamas, slippers and toilet things, there were listed writing materials and note-books, about a dozen books which he intended to re-read and an equal number he hadn't yet read, several bottles of eau-de-Cologne and toilet water and tins of talcum powder. Above all, I was to be sure that his bedside lamp accompanied him. In his experience, hospital bedside lights were quite hopeless: he must have his own – one of those long, rangy, many-angled things which you can tilt in any direction you want.

In spite of our request that we should not be bothered by newspapers, the telephone rang almost continually, though it now only sounded at the far end of the flat from where Gilbert slept. We had not announced that he was going into hospital. It had been decided to wait until we knew how long he would be there. Even then, we hoped we should be able to keep quiet the fact that he was in the London Clinic. We knew that, once it was known, their switchboard would be jammed with telephone inquiries. All the staff of the Clinic, from the porters upwards and downwards, had been instructed to deny that he was there, or expected there, if asked. The driver and attendant of the ambulance had been told the same. So I had to be very evasive indeed with telephone calls from the press reporters, who knew his B B C engagements, too, had now been cancelled.

The patient slept fitfully all the afternoon and it was a relief, when the ambulance arrived, to feel that he would soon be in the hands of those well equipped to take the responsibility of his illness. But Gilbert himself hated the idea so much that Mrs. Clarke and I were almost in tears when, at the last moment, he pleaded with the doctors to let him stay at home. Fortunately, the doctors were not so moved. His own doctor went with him in the ambulance and a few minutes later, as arranged, I followed in a taxi, carrying the bedside lamp and one or two things I had been unable to pack.

I was held up by traffic and it was some time before I got to Devonshire Place and the front door of the Clinic. Carrying the bed-side light tucked under my arm like a jointed toy giraffe, I went over to the porter's desk and asked on what floor I would find Mr. Gilbert Harding's room. The porter looked blank. 'There's no Mr. Harding here,' he said and took a step towards me, as if ready to hustle me out. 'But I'm his secretary. I know he's here. I saw him off from home in the ambulance.' 'Well, that still doesn't mean he's here,' replied the porter woodenly. 'And, in any case, if you're a secretary, what do you want with all that photographer's outfit?' For a moment, I thought one of us must be unhinged, until I realized that he was staring at the lamp under my arm. Indeed, it did look something like equipment for flash photography. When I explained it, the porter was at last convinced and told me where to find the Sister in charge. It was a maddening delay, but I realized it meant that the porter was, in fact, doing exactly as he had been told – and doing it well.

When I got to Gilbert's room, he was already in bed, well propped up with pillows and being fussed over by several nurses. His eyes were closed and he looked very ill. When he heard my voice, his eyes opened. 'Where the hell have you been?' he snarled. 'You were sup-posed to follow at once in a taxi and here I've been waiting for you for over an hour.' I saw no point in telling him how untrue this was. Instead I thought to amuse him by recounting the story of the incident with the porter. He was not amused. It merely confirmed, he said, what he had always felt about hospitals and nursing homes.

Then, 'Are you going to stand there all night, hopping from one foot to another, or do you intend to do anything about having my light fixed?' Naturally, the plug already on the lamp would not fit the socket by his bed. Of course, the Clinic's maintenance men had gone off duty and the shops were shut. Trying to be helpful, a nurse said soothingly, 'Well, after all, you won't really need a reading lamp tonight, will you, Mr. Harding? You'll soon be fast asleep.' Gilbert's retort ensured that the kindly nurse would never again try to jolly that particular patient along!

Throughout the time he was in the Clinic, I tried to remind myself continually of his almost neurotic fear of hospitals and how much it must be affecting his spirits and his temper. I didn't always succeed. For during his stay, I visited him twice, sometimes three times a day and on almost every occasion he vented his phobia on me in bursts of ill-temper.

That evening I was soon sent away so that he could be x-rayed and then settled for the night with a strong sedative. I went back to Cadogan Place to try to tidy up a little of the chaos we had left behind. Mrs. Clarke was already clearing up the sitting-room. Her first words horrified me. 'Did that reporter from the *Daily Sketch* find you at the Clinic?' she asked. 'He came here about half an hour ago. I told him Mr. Harding had been taken to the Clinic and you were there with him.' Poor Mrs. Clarke! She was the only one we had forgotten to tell that the whole thing must be kept absolutely secret. Within a few minutes the reporter was back at the front door. The Clinic, he said, had denied that Gilbert Harding was there. 'That's because he *isn't* there,' I said. But, obviously, it was no longer any use denying that he had left Cadogan Place. I said he had been taken to a London nursing home. Again the telephone began to ring every few minutes. It was midnight before it stopped for long enough to allow me to get ready to go home, and then it was only because I had asked the specialist to issue a bulletin to the press. He announced that Gilbert was already responding to treatment, that his condition was satisfactory and that a further bulletin would be issued the following day at noon.

When, the next day, after I had called at Cadogan Place to open the post and collect more things Gilbert had asked for, shopped at the greengrocer's, the chemist's and called at the library, I reached the Clinic at ten o'clock. Gilbert seemed no better – and, certainly, no happier. It seemed that nothing I had brought was what he had asked for. I had taken apples: he had quite distinctly said he wanted pears. The books I had collected from the library were certainly not from his list. And so on. Fortunately, I was too tired to argue – and he too ill to continue for long. He drifted to sleep again. When I called again, in the late afternoon, I was told that he wasn't responding to treatment quite so well as he had done earlier. He looked weaker and seemed exhausted.

The following morning he seemed even worse, after a very restless night. But he still managed a grumble or two. A few hours later he appeared very, very ill indeed. But it was nevertheless a great shock when the specialist took me aside and said Gilbert's position was now critical and any further deterioration within the next twenty-four hours would almost certainly prove fatal.

CHAPTER FIVE

BANANA BOAT TO JAMAICA

ONE of the things that worried me about the sudden gravity of Gilbert's health was that his mother had not been well for some time and I was afraid of her being shocked by the unexpected news. I telephoned a friend of hers in Hereford to ask her to break it before Mrs. Harding should see the newspapers. When I had spoken to the friend I was even more anxious. She told me Mrs. Harding, too, was in a nursing home.

It seemed that for some time she had been living on the lightest of diets to palliate what was assumed to be a gastric ulcer. Gradually she had weakened and had finally been quite pleased to accept the doctor's suggestion of expert nursing. She shared with her elder sister, Edith King, the house in Hereford which had once been the home of their parents. But Edith was not strong enough to do the nursing so a room was found in a local nursing home. Then, on the evening I learned that Gilbert had reached a crisis. I had a telephone call from Hereford to say that Mrs. Harding, too, was causing considerable anxiety. In the last few days she had appreciably weakened, but at least she had not asked to see any newspapers, so she knew nothing of her son's plight.

That particular danger did not last long, however. Before twelve of the critical twenty-four hours had passed, Gilbert began to show signs of improvement. On the Sunday morning, when I telephoned to the Clinic, I was told I could not visit him that morning but I might come briefly in the evening. When I arrived, they told me he had certainly turned the corner and the danger was passed, though he was still very weak. Sister said I might see him for just a few moments, but I must not tire him.

Weak he must have been, but Gilbert was still able to tell me,

78

in remarkably healthy language, of some of the outrages which had been perpetrated against him in the past twenty-four hours. The worst had been the bed-pan! The doctor had faithfully promised him, before Gilbert agreed to go to the Clinic, that he would be allowed to go to the lavatory. 'I refuse to have that offensive utensil in the room again,' he tried to shout. 'I'll throw it at the next nurse who brings it in!' He announced that he must leave the place and get back home.

'Yes, yes,' I said soothingly, afraid he would collapse again in front of me. 'The moment you're well enough, I'm sure the doctor will let you come home.'

'Well enough? What chance,' Gilbert demanded, 'have I got to get well here? They're just a lot of bloody busybodies. They fuss and fret and fiddle about with pills and potions and pricks every other minute of the day. They keep the lights on so that I can't sleep and, if I do manage to doze off, they wake me up to give me a sleeping draught. If I stay here another couple of days they'll be the death of me!'

There was a tap on the door. One of the nurses came in to suggest that 'Mr. Harding might be tired. Sister thinks you should leave now.' It was the visitor who was tired. Mr. Harding was only just getting into his stride: his face fell as I meekly said, 'Yes, of course, Nurse. Good night, Mr. Harding,' and followed her from the room. It wasn't really fair, for I knew that he was just beginning to enjoy himself.

During the time Gilbert was in the Clinic, the doctors issued regular bulletins with which we could answer newspaper inquiries. At first they used words like 'serious', 'severe' and 'concern' but as soon as the crisis was over the phrasing settled down to something like 'making satisfactory progress'. Not unnaturally, perhaps, this sudden change of tone made the more cynical reporters believe that his illness had been exaggerated. One story, in particular, bitterly hurt Gilbert.

His place on *What's My Line?* had been taken by Robert Morley. On the day after Morley's first appearance – and only four days after Gilbert had been taken to the Clinic – Bob Keston wrote in his column in the *Evening Standard*: 'After watching Robert Morley perform so well in his place, I wonder whether Gilbert Harding's illness will last as long as originally expected.' Of the many unkind things written about him, this upset Gilbert the most. He had known Keston in Canada and Gilbert seemed to think that the writer was trying to settle an old score. If so, he certainly succeeded. I hope he never knew how well.

But people – close friends and doctors, as well as the public – were always astounded by Gilbert's power of recovery. The staff of the London Clinic were baffled by his extraordinary change at the critical period. Two years later, at the Brompton Hospital, the experts were similarly amazed. Gilbert's heart was in an almost fatal condition – 'in failure' the specialist called it – and, day after day, the drug dosage had to be increased until it reached much more than double the amount that was considered the absolute maximum. But apparently without effect. Then, despite the drugs, his condition began to get worse and even the specialist despaired. Quite suddenly the drugs seemed to begin to work. Within a very few hours he was out of danger and, two weeks later, was up and about again as usual.

Almost the same situation – perhaps even more hopeless – occurred in 1959 when Gilbert was in the University College Hospital with a return of the same heart condition. This time it was aggravated by the fact that his kidneys, because of the shortage of oxygen in his blood, ceased to function. Already, when he was admitted to hospital, his life was in danger. He was kept continuously in an oxygen tent and given massive doses of every known drug that might affect his condition. As many as three bulletins a day were issued to the press, each growing slightly graver in tone. Almost all hope had been abandoned when, once more, the miracle happened. It was Easter Saturday. On the morning of that day it seemed he would not last through it. But by the evening it was quite obvious that he had firmly dragged himself round another corner. It was obvious, too, that the bulletin for the Sunday papers must be carefully phrased lest the reporters, once again, should feel they had been hoodwinked. After a lot of thought, I rang the Press Association (one of the big agencies which supplies all newspapers with news) and gave them this: 'The slight change for the better noted in Mr. Harding's condition earlier today has been maintained and has turned into a marked improvement.' But that did not stave off inquiries. Telephone calls from the Sunday newspapers kept Joan Smith and me from our beds until very late.

But the stay at the London Clinic was, of course, my first experience of this kind of situation. It was a very trying one. As he began to recover, my days became breathless. Very often I had to go to the Clinic three times a day and my visits seldom lasted less than

An informal snap of Gilbert with Nancy Spain on the banana boat.

'Mr Harding, a Hereford dove-breeder', after unsuccessfully challenging the panel of *What's My Line?* Just returned from Jamaica, he gives Eamonn Andrews a souvenir.

With Hermione Gingold.

Questioned by John
Freeman during the
controversial *Face to Face*
programme on B B C
television.
(*B B C photograph*)

two hours. Each morning I went first to Cadogan Place to open the mail and extract those letters I thought Gilbert might want to see, hurrying to get away to the Clinic before Sister or one of the nurses apologetically phoned to say Mr. Harding was wondering if I were coming or not. It might be that I had to call at one or two shops to get something he had asked for the previous evening. It seldom took less than half an hour by taxi, even when the traffic was not particularly heavy.

Sometimes I was greeted with, 'Ah well, now. We finally have the honour of a visit from Mr. Storey. I do hope you haven't got heart failure from hurrying!'

Sometimes it was, 'Ah, Roger, good. Glad you got here so early. Now I must have . . .'

It seemed to me that he spent all the time between my visits making lists of what he wanted. There were books by the dozen, many of them obscure and difficult to obtain. He wanted fruit which was certain to be out of season and it involved half an hour on the telephone or a visit to half a dozen shops to find it. He didn't like the tea the Clinic used, nor the coffee. I had to keep buying new blends of each until he was satisfied. But I thanked God the doctor kept him on a rigid diet or I might have spent even more time in Soho groceries and the big food stores.

So off I would go, shopping and hunting, to be back by his bedside at two o'clock. Then, perhaps towards four o'clock, I would take a taxi back to the flat, collect anything he needed and try to sort some more of the mail before returning at six.

The mail was almost unbelievable. Christmas was getting near and it seemed as though every other person in the country had decided to send him a card. I asked the staff of *The People* not to send on any of the hundreds of cards they had received for him there, but from the B B C on three or four occasions they arrived by the sackful. They became almost a nightmare to me. I got up earlier and earlier and went to bed later and later in my efforts at least to open them all. Gilbert's reactions were thoroughly mixed. His ready vein of sentiment, his mistrust of easy popularity, his hatred of 'a cash Christmas', all needed expression at once.

'Look at them,' he said, letting a pile flutter from his hands all over the bed and the floor, 'all these throbbing good wishes from people who never met me in their lives. If they had, they wouldn't want to wish me well, I know. See this one? It must have cost some

D

good soul about two shillings – look at all that nasty glitter on the Christmas tree! Horrible!' Yet sometimes he would turn them over one by one and study the messages of kindness and encouragement without a word.

It would have taken more than Christmas cards to make him cheerful then. As he grew stronger, he became more miserable at his confinement. His grumbles and complaints grew louder. For me, almost every visit was torment, particularly in anticipation. Yet I could go home and leave him there. The staff of the Clinic, on duty for hours at a time, maintained continually their efforts to please him – with no apparent result whatever. Though no hint of it ever appeared, they must have been as anxious for the patient to leave them as he was himself. He discussed endlessly, it seemed, plans for his discharge. He elaborated a plan to be home for Christmas at Cadogan Place, with a male nurse to care for him and watch over the pills and potions and his diet. To me the doctor insisted the plan was absurd. Even if we could turn the flat at Cadogan Place into a Clinic-in-miniature, with day and night nurses and all the necessary equipment, he still dare not let Gilbert leave.

So the time came when I had to pass on this decision to the hopeful patient. The scene that followed made all his previous tantrums seem like mere peevishness. He unleashed his fury in a storm of abuse at everyone concerned with his plight – but most of all on me. In a wild flight of fancy he insisted that I must have some personal, malicious motive in refusing to arrange for his return home. Day after day, despite my puzzled denials, he returned to this accusation and, though I knew that a sick man is not always a reasonable one, I began to wonder if I worked for a lunatic – or, perhaps, if he were trying to make me believe so. My own Christmas plans provoked a terrible outburst. I had arranged to go home to Yorkshire but, in all honesty, I told Gilbert that, if it would be of any help, I would stay in London instead.

'Oh noble Roger! Oh what a sacrifice was there! Now we see the ultimate martyrdom of the faithful. What a dreadful thing – that I should ever deny any man the overwhelming joy of deliverance from the tedious horrors of a sick employer. Such abnegation! Such munificence! No, no, let it never be said that I took advantage of such generosity. Go to Yorkshire. Go and feast on the riotous delights of Christmas in Muddlecombe-on-the-Ouse. Who am I to deny you such pagan jollity?'

I stood there for a moment, trembling and tongue-tied. Then I almost ran from the room. But later I felt I must make the same suggestion to the doctor, in case it would, in fact, be wiser for me to stay within call over the holiday. 'I don't,' said the doctor, 'want to have two patients on my hands. If you can't get a few days' rest, that's what I shall have.' I didn't argue with him.

The doctor's patience, too, must have been hard-tried, but before Gilbert and the nursing staff he maintained his calm detachment. Only once did the mask slip a little. One day I saw him as I went in to visit the patient. A few moments later I met him again as I was leaving. 'That was a very short visit,' he said inquiringly. I explained that I had apparently forgotten a book which Gilbert said he had particularly asked me to bring from Cadogan Place. 'As you're going back to the flat,' said the doctor, 'perhaps you had better bring his favourite golliwog back with you, too.' I wondered if the doctor was going mad under the strain. He smiled. 'Every child has its favourite toy. I can't imagine your employer is any exception.'

Between visits to the Clinic and in my 'spare moments' when I wasn't fetching books or fruit or coffee for Gilbert, I did his Christmas shopping – more books, record tokens, wine, scent and hampers of good things. Two of them might have surprised the nursing staff at the Clinic who knew only his sulks and furies. They were sent to complete strangers – a hamper containing a complete Christmas dinner, with chocolates, nuts and a bottle of fine port to a couple of old-age-pensioners in Camberwell, and a parcel of toys and games, crackers and sweets to a family in Devon whose father was spending the holiday in hospital after a severe operation. From among the many letters wishing him a swift recovery, he had found these two from people suffering very much more than he, and at once determined to try to help a little.

After pleadings, arguments and threats, Gilbert finally got the doctor to agree that he would be well enough to leave the Clinic immediately after Christmas. It was arranged that I should collect him in a hired car at ten o'clock on my first day back from Yorkshire. I paid him a final visit just before I left for home. He was at his most friendly, charming best, wishing me a happy Christmas, sending his love to my mother and telling me warmly to enjoy myself. 'Now just you get away and forget all about me and my boorishness for a few days. I do apologize, Podge, for all the trouble

I have been giving you.' I travelled north feeling exhausted, but much lighter in heart. But I didn't forget all about him. I put through a call to the Clinic on Christmas Day and was connected to the phone at his bedside. 'I rang to wish you as happy a Christmas as possible, Mr. Harding. I do hope you're feeling much better.' 'Happy Christmas, indeed!' came the snorted reply, followed – for six minutes at my expense – by a volley of furious grumbles.

On the way home, I had read in the evening newspaper the most recent bulletin on my employer's illness. They reported that he was making a good recovery and planned to return home immediately after Christmas. They added: 'It is understood that Mr. Roger Storey, Mr. Harding's secretary, is travelling to Yorkshire today, to spend Christmas with his parents.' I felt all that remained now was to see my name in the Court Circular! I don't know whether I was more embarrassed than flattered when, travelling back to London by an overnight train, I was asked by the sleeping-car attendant if I were 'that Mr. Roger Storey who is Gilbert Harding's secretary?'

Back in London, I was immediately plunged into the flurry of his return to Cadogan Place. Though the time of Gilbert's departure had not been announced, there were already a dozen or more photographers and reporters waiting outside the front door when I arrived at the Clinic early that morning. Thanks to Matron's foresight, it had been arranged that the car should come to the back door, which led into a yard protected by a wide double gate. Gilbert, warmly wrapped up, and I, loaded with paraphernalia, were packed into one of the service lifts and were away in the car and back at the flat a little after ten o'clock. Before we left, Gilbert had effusively thanked Matron for the care and kindness he had received. Then he suggested that it was unkind to let the pressmen wait interminably and proposed that, after we were well on our way, they should be told that he had gone because he didn't feel well enough for pictures and interviews.

But we were still innocent of the thoroughness of news editors. We drew up at the door of the Cadogan Place flats to find almost as many newspapermen, with cameras and note-books, clustered there. 'Poor creatures,' said Gilbert. 'Hadn't we better ask them in?' I was thoroughly alarmed. 'I'm sure you aren't strong enough to stand it,' I said. 'Please don't.' So we bustled through them and hurriedly shut the door on their pleas. But, even as we did so, the telephone was ringing. One newspaper after another asked for a 'back home again' story and picture. Finally, I arranged for an agency to send one man to take several pictures and make them available to any newspaper which was still interested.

One of the things that had naturally worried Gilbert during his stay at the Clinic was the expense. In addition to the bare fee for just being there, there were the doctor's and specialist's accounts to be paid and the money lost from cancelled engagements had to be taken into the reckoning. In all, we worked out that his twelve days there had cost something like five hundred pounds. There had been just one saving factor. When Gilbert was beginning to recover, he had been asked by the editor of *Illustrated* to write an article on his illness, accompanied by photographs. The fee they offered would go a good way towards the cost of the treatment. Gilbert was enthusiastic. We sought – and, surprisingly, received – the permission of the doctor, the matron and the governors of the Clinic. The article was written, the pictures taken, and we were told it would appear in January.

Unfortunately, we had innocently overlooked something apparently much more important than the medical profession. As a regular contributor to *Picture Post*, Gilbert should have consulted the editor of that journal before accepting the offer of *Illustrated*. And, quite obviously, his permission would not have been forthcoming, since the two periodicals were rivals. On the day that 'My Confounded Illness' appeared in *Illustrated*, a brisk and bitter storm broke about our heads. The editor of *Picture Post* was shocked and staggered by Gilbert's duplicity; it had not occurred to him that it might be sheer innocence.

As Gilbert had said in his *Illustrated* article, the use of penicillin and other antibiotics had ensured so quick a recovery that it was hard to admit the need for convalescence. Gilbert didn't, in fact, admit it. After spending just one day quietly at home, he was out and about again as usual. He returned to *What's My Line?* the following Monday and was given a warm-hearted reception by press and public. But the next day he travelled to Hereford to see his mother.

During his illness, I had gradually broken to him the news that his mother was in hospital and gravely ill, though I had done my utmost to allay his worry about her. Now that he was free again, his immediate thought was to visit her. It was to be the last time that she could still recognize him. She was so obviously sinking that he returned to London very deeply unhappy. He visited her again twice after that and he was with her when, on 2nd February, 1954, she died of inoperable cancer.

Although he was prepared for it, his mother's death came as a terrible blow to Gilbert. He shared with Mrs. Harding a strange, perhaps rather enviable, attitude to death. He had often told me that when his father died, during Gilbert's early childhood, the widow had shocked her family by ordering that her husband's grave should be levelled, without a headstone, so that no reminder of it should remain. 'The body,' she had said, 'should be forgotten: the spirit needs no memorial.' Gilbert equally shocked many of his relations by arranging for his mother's funeral to be held in strict privacy. He dreaded publicity in such an intimate emotion. Only two or three close relatives were present. And though, within a few weeks, he seemed to have recovered from the sadness of her death, his nearest friends realized that it would be many years before his sorrow healed.

The arrangements for his mother's funeral had, in fact, followed quite closely upon the discussions of his own. While he was in the Clinic, before his recovery had become assured, Gilbert had seemed to take great pleasure in detailing his own obsequies.

'It will all be up to you, Roger,' he had pointed out. 'Don't waste money on pomp and ceremony. Just get me dug into the ground at the nearest cemetery. Paupers can be buried quite cheaply by the local authority – mind you don't spend more than that. If I've got any money to leave, don't fritter it on a funeral.' Over the years, those instructions were repeated to me again and again until, one day, he suddenly, and audibly, realized that whoever was responsible for burying him would obviously please themselves how they did it. 'I'm talking like a fool. I might just as well save my breath,' he decided.

With his mother's death, Gilbert could no longer call Hereford home. Miss King, Gilbert's 'Aunt Edie' now found the house much too big for herself alone and though, for a time, they discussed letting part of it, in the end they agreed that Miss King should move to a home for old people just outside the city. Later she moved to a nursing home in Hereford. There she still lives, with the companionship of kindly people and the added comfort of small extravagances made possible by her nephew. The house was sold. Most of the furniture was put in store. And Gilbert began to revive again an old dream of buying a house of his own in London.

But while we discussed house-hunting, we planned what Gilbert rightly felt to be a long overdue holiday. Travel books and brochures were scanned and discussed and piled around. They were joined by lists from house agents, which arrived in daily dozens. So on our way to survey a house in Chelsea, we discussed the climate of Spain; in a taxi to Hampstead or Campden Hill, we talked of the hotels of Austria and the fjords of Sweden. Gilbert decided finally on complete relaxation and the near-solitude of a round trip to Jamaica on a banana boat. He would be several days at sea, stay for three days at King's House with the Governor, Sir Hugh Foot, with whom he had been very friendly at Cambridge, and then make the return voyage to Liverpool – in all, just a little over three weeks, leaving in early March. With the holiday settled and still no suitable house, Gilbert decided he would settle for a flat, so long as it had no less than six rooms and 'the usual offices'.

The pace increased. As we rushed around from flat to flat, Gilbert would take an hour or two off to buy clothes or luggage for his holiday or to refresh himself in any convenient public house. He raced up to Hereford to make sure his aunt was comfortably settled in her new home, made several recordings for the B B C, dictated his *People* article for the following Sunday, wrote enough material to keep the *Picture Post* column going during his absence – and made and signed his will. It implied a rather fearful permanence in my job, for he bequeathed me five hundred pounds. Only in the final week did he learn that Nancy Spain and her friend, Joan Werner Laurie, would be on the same ship for the outward voyage to Jamaica.

At last, breathless and exhausted, I delivered my even more worn employer to Euston and saw him off on the boat train. So did the Station Master, in his top hat and carrying his white gloves. Gilbert and I did not dare to ask, nor did we ever find out, if he was there for that purpose or whether some important person was travelling at that time. We did not really suppose that such an exalted official would bother to appear for a mere television personality. As the train drew out, I turned back to my long, long list of allegedly suitable houses and flats for inspection and to the wild chaos and confusion of my office.

I began by opening all the Christmas cards and letters – sacks of them. Though it was past Christmas and the recipient away, I felt it would have been ungracious not to open them. The cards

I finally, with the help of Mrs. Clarke, packed into several large cartons for despatch to various charitable organizations. Many of the letters came from Roman Catholics and contained religious medals or scapulars. Most of these I acknowledged, but I was relieved to find many of them anonymous. In 1929, some time after he left Cambridge, Gilbert had been converted to the Roman Church and this fact was becoming more widely known. Over the years an increasing proportion of his fan letters came from members of that faith, seeing in him, perhaps, one who had the ability and opportunity to speak for their Church in this country. Yet it seemed sad to me – a man of no defined religious views, that Gilbert, having taken what was obviously a most important step in his spiritual life, did not come to find in his religion the emotional stability and satisfaction I imagined it should bring. Occasionally he confided in me that he sometimes almost regretted having left the Anglican Church and so crossed a bridge from his early youth. More often he took a very strong anti-Protestant view, deriding the empty churches of the Anglicans and the Nonconformists. He gave generously and often to the Catholic cause. In spite of his worldly life, he had constant invitations to important Roman Catholic functions and more than one priest was his good friend.

With the Christmas mail out of the way, peace was in sight. But then another whirlwind rose. Gilbert had been on his way to Jamaica for four or five days when the newspapers began to hint at a romance between him and Nancy Spain. I knew nothing of it until one morning Mrs. Clarke greeted me with one of her classic remarks. 'Well, Storey' – her form of address for me ranged from Sir, Mr. Storey, Mr. Roger, Roger, to just plain Storey – 'what do you think of Nancy for Mum?' She produced the *Daily Sketch*. Simon Ward's column asked:

'Is Gilbert Harding thinking of marrying? I hear talk of a romance between the irascible 47-year-old T V bachelor and novelist Nancy Spain, who is 37. Right now they are on a not-so-slow banana boat, the *Matina*, headed for Jamaica and a holiday. They met at Liverpool Docks to go on board together. And when they got on board they went to see the captain for a chat.

Before she left London, I'm told, Nancy said to friends: "I am considering marrying Gilbert." It would be a fiery combination – the quick-tempered Gilbert and sharp-witted bohemian Nancy, who even wears slacks to the theatre.'

By the following day every national newspaper had taken up the story and they devoted a great deal of space to conjecture and to cables exchanged between themselves and the allegedly romantic couple. To the *Daily Mirror* cable asking if romance was, in fact, in the air, they had sent a joint reply:

> *Mirror, mirror in the Street,*
> *What next? You really have us beat.*
> *The Captain's name is Frederick Inch,*
> *And though he has a splendid winch*
> *And lots of hope*
> *And yards of rope,*
> *Alas, the law says he may not,*
> *However willing, tie the knot.*
> *If you did not know that before,*
> *See Merchant Shipping Act of '94.*

To which the same newspaper replied:

> *The question was: Are you to wed?*
> *Not what the heck the skipper said.*
> *There's land ahoy, and churches, too;*
> *Where to wed is up to you.*
> *Please answer either no or yes.*
> *No matter which, we say 'God bless'.*

This time they got a definite answer from Gilbert:

> *Alas, in spite of jolly verse,*
> *The answer's short and somewhat terse.*
> *The rumour's heaven, the dream divine,*
> *But wedlock is still not my line.*
> *And so, dear folk, these facts being so,*
> *The dreary answer's 'No, no, no'.*

Though Gilbert returned from his holiday as heart-whole as he left, this rumour was revived from time to time over the next eighteen months. Later, in the summer, he and Nancy Spain appeared together in a television programme *Who Said That?* in which quotations had to be identified and then discussed. One was about marriage. When Gilbert said that he wished he were married,

D*

Nancy immediately capped it with 'I wouldn't mind marrying you.' Again the newspapers pounced and we were pestered with 'Is there anything in it?' Gilbert firmly announced that he liked Nancy much too much to ask her to consider living with a grumpy, unpleasant person as himself.

And Nancy had already, in her account of the 'romance' on board, written of Gilbert: 'He talked steadily from one side of the Atlantic to the other, mowing down the opposition with every trick of the orator's art. Any word I tried to cram in edgeways was cast aside like an under-sized trout. Here and now I put on record, if ever again I share my breakfast, my hangover, my tropic moon with any gentleman . . . he's got to let me do some of the talking.'

But one thing puzzled me much more than the newspaper rumours. It was Gilbert's extravagance in sending me cables. The first – and shortest – said: 'Have jolliest time denying rumour I am marrying Nancy Spain Stop What next?' After that, they kept coming. Sometimes there were even two in one day, long and verbose, without much attempt at condensation or 'cablese'. Oddest of all, very few of the messages were of any importance at all – except for two or three which told of some house or flat that Nancy had told him was available. While admiring Nancy's memory for such matters, I began to wish it were less ready or more efficient, for out of her suggestions one was the size of a shoe-box, two had already been taken and the owner of the fourth had no intention of letting or selling.

Not until Gilbert had been home for six weeks was the mystery of the lavish cabling solved. He received a bill from the wireless telegraph company for over twenty pounds.

'Rubbish! Nonsense!' he said when I showed it to him. 'I don't owe them a penny. All the cables I sent to you were prepaid.' I protested that since I hadn't cabled to him, that would not, in fact, have been possible. 'Oh, don't be so moronic, Podge! They were all newspaper left-overs.'

Poor Gilbert, what a horrid awakening he had. When the press had sent him cabled inquiries about Nancy, they had hopefully requested long, pre-paid replies. But when, for example, the *Daily Sketch* had suggested a fifty-word reply, Gilbert had simply answered, 'Much regret must utterly deny rumour. Harding,' and blandly sent me a 43-word cable on the assumption that otherwise the *Sketch*'s good money would go to waste.

It was a long and bitter dispute with Cable and Wireless but, at last, when they pointed out that, if Gilbert didn't pay the bill, the *Matina*'s wireless operator would be obliged to, he gave in and sent his cheque.

Whenever Gilbert went abroad after that his cables to me were very few and very, very terse.

CHAPTER SIX

THE PUBLIC'S PROPERTY

I⊤ was while Gilbert was away in Jamaica and I had to deal single-handed with the Christmas mail and all the hundreds of letters about his illness, that I began to get some real foretaste of celebrity's fan-mail. Though over the years I gradually ceased to be surprised at the number of people who will write to someone they have never met, I could still occasionally be astonished at the tone of some of the letters that began 'Dear Gilbert . . .'

The volume of letters varied, of course. Most of those concerning his newspaper and magazine work went to the publishers' offices and were mainly answered there. But letters addressed to him about his B B C programmes were all passed on to me and many people, later, just addressed their letters to 'Gilbert Harding, Brighton'. These, too, were invariably delivered.

Viewers of *What's My Line?* wrote in their hundreds – either to congratulate him on an intelligent guess or to revile him for an outburst of impatience or bad manners. Naturally, others wrote to say his guess was inspired by fore-knowledge or that his bad temper was entirely justified. Listeners to *Round Britain Quiz* wrote to complain that one or other team had been awarded too few or too many marks or to say that, though they enjoyed the programme, they knew all the answers long before the experts. *Twenty Questions* brought in even more letters, about half of them adding that the audience should be dropped because it was a noisy nuisance and the other half applauding the added excitement caused by the audible participation of the crowd in the studio.

But many of Gilbert's fans wrote to him quite regularly, as though he were a close friend. We tried always to acknowledge letters, however briefly, and most of these constant correspondents were content with that, but there were some cases which could not be dealt with in that way.

One of his distant letter-writing fans became a real friend. Mrs. Bowling who lives at Westhoughton, in Lancashire, had been writing to him for some time before I became his secretary and he was always happy to read her friendly letters. When an engagement in a stage version of *Twenty Questions* took him to Bolton, he arranged to meet her, and she turned out to be exactly the kind, motherly woman he had expected from her correspondence. After that first meeting, she always visited Gilbert, either in London or Brighton, whenever she came south for a holiday. Gilbert's mother used to knit for him; now Mrs. Bowling did so. She kept him constantly supplied with beautifully made cardigans, pullovers and scarves. She also sent him home-made jams and pickles and supplies of dusters, glass cloths and other 'soft goods' which she thought might be useful. I was included in her generosity, too. When she found out that I had a flat of my own, I often got my own parcel of tea towels, pillow cases and dusters, despite my protests that I didn't deserve them, but by that time she was so used to my answering her letters when my employer was away that she had drawn me into her warm friendship as closely as she had Gilbert.

One Christmas Gilbert said, in his *People* column, that he would be giving his small friends and god-children a traditional Christmas stocking – and that the stockings would be knitted from dishcloth cotton by Mrs. Bowling. Forgetting, as usual, his news-value, he mentioned that she lived in Westhoughton. Northern newspaper reporters ferreted her out and pestered her, day after day, for a story. Several of them carried a picture and a few paragraphs and Mrs. Bowling was very distressed lest 'Mr. Harding should think I wanted publicity'. In fact, Mr. Harding was furious with himself for having caused her so much embarrassment and we did our utmost to convince her of it.

Another good 'pen pal' of Gilbert's was a Mrs. Ashton, who lived in the Midlands. They had the same birthday – 5th June – and she never failed to send him a home-made cake or some other gift then or at Christmas. But she mentioned in one of her letters that her sight was failing and a few months later she dictated a letter saying that she was totally blind. Gilbert had always arranged for flowers to be delivered to her on 'their' birthday and at Christmas: from that day he always took care to order the most sweet-scented bouquets, so that she might still appreciate them. Until

1958 she somehow kept up the correspondence, but that year, when 5th June came round, there was no present for Gilbert and no acknowledgement of his flowers. After a short time we wrote to ask if all was well, but there was no reply. Then we sent a letter addressed simply to 'The Occupier' at her address. When there was still no response we concluded that Mrs. Ashton must have died and, for a long time, Gilbert regretted that he had had no opportunity to make her last months happier or more comfortable.

A correspondence that moved him even more deeply was the letters he exchanged with a little girl, Carol, who lived in a south London suburb. Carol first wrote to Gilbert when she read that he had a Siamese kitten. She wrote of her own Siamese and other pets, and so the pen-friendship started. More than once in her letters Carol mentioned that she had been too ill to go to school, and when she wrote that she might have to go into hospital for the fourth or fifth time, Gilbert became alarmed. He wrote to her parents to ask what was the matter. I have seldom seen him more shocked and distressed than he was when he read her father's reply. Carol had leukaemia, and her parents knew the disease was incurable. The doctors had given her only a few more months. He assured Gilbert that by continuing to write to her he was doing as much as anyone could to help.

After that the letters became increasingly difficult to write as the time ran out. Previously, from time to time, Gilbert had sent Carol small gifts. When, that summer, the time came for her to go into hospital, he sent her a doll. And a few weeks later we heard from her father that Carol was dead.

Many children wrote to Gilbert, and though in most cases the 'friendship' soon died for lack of any real subject of common interest – either to the child or Gilbert – he always enjoyed hearing from them. One of the most charming letters he received came from a small boy in Salisbury who obviously didn't expect a reply since he gave no address. It so delighted me that Gilbert said: 'Well, you had better keep it. You can use it in the book you will be writing about the horrors of working for me.'

I understand that the copyright of a letter lies with the writer of it, so I can only quote the permission of the recipient to reproduce it, in its original grammar, spelling and punctuation:

'Dear Mr. Harding, I was going to write before but I was not allowed to but no one will see this. Its a shame you are on so late you should come on Childrens hour which would be nice. Mummie said Gilbert Harding is coming on again. Jolly good show Gran said. What time oh late said Mummie so I shant see him and she sniffed. Gran said got a cold dear? This morning they were talking again. Mummie said well any way he is rude not writing his name for that woman when he was having his dinner. Gran said, Rubbish why shouldnt he have his meal in pece. Silly woman excepting him to bob up and down bad for the tummy. Then Mummie said I except the dog is like him snappy. Dear girl said Gran one must approach animals with respect same as humans. I hope the dog is well and you both havnt got a cold this wether. Gran and me are going to potter she calls it. Its lovely we go to the Cathedral or to the museum and then to lunch.

With love from Jeremy.

P.S. Mum said you dont care for children.'

But there were other letters which proved most embarrassing. One correspondent – call her Mrs. Oliphant – lived in north London. Her first fan letter received the usual brief acknowledgement. But this did not deter her. She wrote again and said, in passing, that she was a widow, but her letter contained some constructive criticism of one of Gilbert's programmes, for which he thanked her. So her letters continued. Then one night, as he left the B B C studio in Regent Street after *Twenty Questions,* a woman waiting at the exit introduced herself as Mrs. Oliphant. After that she was regularly in the audience and they often exchanged a few words. But gradually the tone of her letters changed. She began to hint that her feelings for him were more than those of an admiring member of the audience. Very soon she declared her deep love for him.

At once Gilbert replied, regretting that he had no wish to know her better and she would do well to forget him at once. He asked that the correspondence and the meetings should cease. But Mrs. Oliphant did answer – with detailed descriptions of her constant dreams of passionate intimacy with her adored Gilbert. Worse, she loudly and proudly began to announce her devotion to the departing audience of *Twenty Questions.* The commissionaires at the studio were warned to refuse her admission, but the first commissionaire brave enough to try to keep her out received a violent kick on the shins and, not unnaturally, declared his intention of calling the police if it should happen again.

This seemed a dreadful last resort, and Gilbert, increasingly horrified by her lewdly amorous letters, wondered how to save her – and himself – from such a painful experience. Unexpectedly, Mrs. Oliphant provided the solution. She wrote a letter on the headed notepaper of her employers – an engineering firm of world-wide repute. At once Gilbert telephoned the staff welfare officer. He was a kindly and sympathetic man and, assured of his understanding, Gilbert told him the story. The welfare officer said he believed he understood and could help Mrs. Oliphant. It seemed that he was right, for he wrote later that he had talked with her and she had asked him to apologize on her behalf. Gilbert never heard from her or saw her again.

There were other women after that who declared their love for Gilbert. But we were constantly cautious in replying. Some grew spiteful when their letters were unanswered, some doggedly continued their sad revelations. But there was one who had been writing to him, and had even met him, some time before I became his secretary. She lived in Surrey and appeared to be quite unable to understand why she should not visit him at any time she wished, bringing, if she desired, her friends and relations with her. She obviously regarded him as public property and when, after having agreed to one or two meetings. Gilbert was 'unable' to make any more appointments she became very angry indeed. And she was convinced that it was my fault: that I was keeping her letters from him. She tried every possible way of circumventing me. She would write to the producer of a programme on which he was to appear, enclosing a letter 'to be given only into Mr. Harding's own hands'. In one of these letters she described me, to Gilbert's never-ending and public delight, as 'that small, dark, monkeyish person'. She telephoned often and angrily. She tracked his movements and appeared, to his dismay, in the audience at any bazaar or exhibition or fête which he opened within reasonable distance of her home.

When Gilbert bought his house in Brighton, it was still within reach of her home. She discovered the address and more than once turned up there without warning. When she was turned away she would go home and at once pick up the telephone, taking it in turn with her relations to abuse him for his lack of manners, his cruelty, his inhumanity. One day I came into the room to find him sitting with the telephone receiver held six inches away from his ear and an expression of deep distaste on his face. He beckoned me over and I, too, could hear the furious clucking sounds.

Suddenly he clapped his hand over the mouthpiece and roared with laughter. 'She sounds like a recently raped turkey,' he spluttered, and I grabbed the receiver to replace it before the poor soul should hear our uncontrollable amusement.

But one woman, who first wrote to Gilbert as a stranger to express her appreciation of any programme which had particularly pleased her, became an invaluable friend to us both. Letters from Miss Diana Roberts were infrequent, friendly, and sensible. On one occasion she said that her work occupied only part of her time, and that only during the summer months: if there were any way in which she could be of use she would be glad to help. Once or twice I acknowledged her letters on Gilbert's behalf, and then she wrote, repeating her offer of help and suggesting that we might meet so that I could satisfy myself that she was an ordinary practical person and no crank. We did meet, and we liked each other at once. Like myself, Diana comes from Yorkshire and, having lived for many years in London, she combined the best characteristics of north and south. At once I realized that she would be an excellent stand-in secretary for Gilbert when I was on holiday.

The following summer, only a few days before I went away for a fortnight, Diana met Gilbert for the first time, and I left her in charge at the flat. When I returned she was already an established – though untitled and unofficial and unpaid – member of the household. From then on Diana was always the first person we turned to in any sort of crisis or emergency. When the daily woman was away ill for two weeks it was Diana who kept the flat running smoothly. Often when Gilbert entertained visitors it was Diana who cut the sandwiches, poured the tea, and acted as hostess. When he was ill in the Brompton Hospital Diana made life tolerable for me by coping with the telephone and the letters and the shopping while I attended the impatient patient.

When the fan mail had been dealt with, there were still the requests for help and advice. Gilbert's weekly column in *The People*, with its enormous circulation, had originally started as a campaign to right the wrongs of little people. Until his health prevented it, he had travelled all over the country visiting people and investigating their complaints of injustice. And so his readers and viewers came to regard him as an expert on problems of housing, law, local government, and education. In fact, of course, he was not. It was the experts who staffed the *People* Advice

Bureau who had provided the knowledge he needed to attack his readers' problems, and the combination of their experience and Gilbert's personality very often proved an irresistible weapon against inhuman officialdom.

But even after the early campaign was over, letters still continued to seek his help and advice. Most of them were passed on to *The People* staff, but for some of them he went to a great deal of trouble, consulting his own solicitor or friends in official positions, to find an answer that could be simply understood, as well as effective.

Most difficult of all to deal with were stories of hardship or ill luck. Wives wrote to tell Gilbert they were in arrears with the rent or hire-purchase payments and did not dare tell their husbands. Husbands wrote to say that their pay packets had been lost or stolen. Old ladies told how, for the first time in twenty years, they had the chance of a holiday by the sea with relations, but had no money for the fare. Old men said that in spite of denying themselves their weekly half-ounce of tobacco and occasional half-pint, they could not afford to buy a coat, but must trudge through wind and rain in a threadbare jacket with the collar turned up.

They made very sad reading and I had no doubt that many of them were entirely genuine. But I did not share Gilbert's optimistic assumption that the percentage from professional writers of begging letters must be very small. He said that for every twenty genuine people he could help, he was quite prepared to be the mug of one dishonest person, and for the first year or so that I was with him he was constantly and, euphemistically, 'lending' money to his correspondents.

Some did quite frankly ask for a loan, which they promised to pay back in instalments over a long period. One woman in Portsmouth actually sent him a small registered package of jewellery as security for a loan of fifty pounds for three months. I persuaded Gilbert to let me take one of the pieces, a small diamond brooch, to a jeweller for valuation. It was worth about two hundred and fifty pounds. I hastily packed the jewels up again and returned them with a polite note saying Gilbert was unable to do as she asked.

My feelings about the begging letters were partly based on a novel I had read, most convincingly describing how a young and healthy man had existed quite comfortably on the money he had raised by writing to rich people in the guise of the disabled father of a large family. They were finally confirmed by a conversation I had with Elizabeth Allan's secretary about our employers' mail. She happened to mention a very sad letter to Miss Allan from a man living in the north whose wife was dying of an incurable disease. Because he had four young children he could not even manage to provide his sick wife with some of the necessities, let alone the luxuries, she needed. Moved by his plight Miss Allan had sent him money. Back at the office I looked out a letter recently addressed to Gilbert. It was from a woman who said that her husband had lost both legs in an accident at work. With four young children to feed and clothe, the inadequate compensation had soon dwindled away and the family was suffering very great hardship. Could Mr. Harding help with a few pounds? I telephoned Elizabeth Allan's secretary for the name and address of the man with the dying wife. They were the same as on the letter I held.

When I told Gilbert, he agreed with me that he should be more cautious in future. We discovered that organizations like the W V S, the Salvation Army, and the British Legion were only too happy to investigate individual cases and to try to give help where it was genuinely needed, so after the case of the legless father of four we often asked their advice. One of the first letters we sent to the W V S made even Gilbert wonder how many times he had been a sucker. It came from Newark, from a woman who said that in her determination to keep her three children always clean and respectable she was left without money to buy winter clothes for herself. Her husband was a factory worker and his small wages did not go far, particularly as they also kept an aged grandmother in the household. It had taken her many weeks to swallow her pride and, for the first time in her life, ask for help. Could Gilbert suggest how she could get the winter coat she so badly needed? The local organizer of the W V S called on the writer, and her report astounded us. There was only one child of school age in the family – a boy of fourteen – but a grown-up son and daughter and the mother worked in the same factory as the father. Their combined earnings amounted to about forty-five pounds a week!

Then there were the abusive letters, most of them anonymous. Even when they bore a name and address they were very seldom answered, though often Gilbert wanted to be more violently offensive in reply. I managed eventually to convince him that it was much better to ignore them, for then the writer would not even know whether or not Gilbert had seen them. Sometimes these communications came in the form of mutilated or decorated photographs of Gilbert, and one of them distressed him so deeply that he never forgot it. It arrived soon after his mother had died. It was a picture of Christ wearing the crown of thorns, but the face had been replaced by Gilbert's own and underneath was written: 'Your mother has gone to Hell. Why don't you join her?'

There were people who wrote asking for photographs and for autographs, and so numerous did these sometimes become that we made it a rule not to comply unless a stamped envelope was enclosed, though I often broke the rule for young children. It surprised me to find how many adults, when asking for autographs, said it was not for themselves but for friends, children or relations. The same thing happened when people approached him in public to ask him to sign a book or a piece of paper. I remember once, when he appeared at the Radio Show, one man said: 'This isn't for me, it's for my wife. She thinks you're wonderful, but personally I can't stand the sight or the sound of you.'

Many of Gilbert's admirers sent him small presents – books, bunches of wild flowers, or something they knew he particularly wanted. If he mentioned in his *People* column his liking for fresh mint sauce, for crusty bread, oak-smoked kippers, or kholrabi, all these things were delivered for days afterwards by the already-burdened postman – many of them in no condition to be eaten. I still recall with nausea one particular box of bloaters, long delayed in the post, which was literally crawling when it reached us. Once, in *Twenty Questions*, he said that he had not seen the Bayeux Tapestries and how much he would like to. Even his most generous fans could not quite satisfy that wish for him, but they sent what they thought was the next best thing: the gifts ranged from cross-stitched pictures of improbable geese flying across impossibly-hued skies to exquisite pieces of *petit point*. On another occasion, when the object was 'a stag beetle', Gilbert said he had never seen one. Within a week he had seen hundreds. A few of those sent him were properly preserved and mounted, but the majority had obviously been freshly caught just to send to him. By the time they arrived, 'fresh' was the last word one could have used about them. A few, however, were so fresh that they were still alive and delightedly escaped from captivity when the package was opened.

Only very rarely did he ever receive threatening letters, but he seldom took action of any kind about them and only in one case did he ever meet what seemed to be the authors. After a television

programme in which he had spoken harshly of Teddy boys he
had a letter signed 'The Bush Boys', promising him 'a good beating-
up' unless (a) he withdrew his remarks in his next television programme and (b) never again entered a certain public house in
'the Bush' (Shepherd's Bush, where the BBC television studios
are). The apology was not, of course, given and Gilbert made
a special point, at the first opportunity, of visiting the forbidden
public house. He was just ordering his drink at the bar when
he realized that four Teddy boys had sidled up and arranged
themselves in couples on each side of him.

'You know what we've come for, don't you?' one of them said
grimly.

'I don't know what you've come for, but I certainly know what
you'll get if you don't move out of my way,' Gilbert answered.

Gilbert's vocabulary of invective was wide, and I am certain that
in the flow of mutual insult which followed he must have swiftly
and easily overcome his opponent. The whole incident suddenly
fizzled out as abruptly as it had started. Gilbert himself did not
tell me of this meeting. I heard the story from the landlord of
the pub a few weeks later. He said he had seen nothing of the
four young men since that night and added, rather wistfully I
thought: 'Until then they had been among my best customers.'

CHAPTER SEVEN

A NEW HOME

THE boat which brought Gilbert back from Jamaica docked at Southampton early one Sunday morning at the end of March 1954, and that evening a Mr. G. Harding, of Hereford – an alleged dove-breeder – challenged the *What's My Line?* panel. He had been away from the programme for three weeks and he was given a vociferous welcome by the audience and by his panel colleagues, who guessed his assumed occupation in record time. This little joke back-fired on Gilbert in a most unexpected way. For several months afterwards, he received letters from would-be dove-breeders who hoped that, from his experience, he might be able to give them advice and information.

Although Gilbert's outbursts of ill-temper and his frequent tetchi-ness were undoubtedly the reason why so many people continued to watch *What's My Line?* week after week, I think the B B C officials had hoped that his brief holiday would make him less irritable on the programme. But it did not seem to have done so. His outbursts continued and when Ron Randell replaced David Nixon on the panel for the last few weeks before the programme was rested for the summer, there was an added excitement for the viewer. Off-screen, Gilbert and Mr. Randell were perfectly friendly towards each other but, on the panel, they occasionally exchanged rather acid remarks and the public, with the help of one or two newspaper columnists, soon built up these exchanges into a state of feud.

The same thing happened more than two years later when Bob Monkhouse was on the panel. One evening Gilbert objected to the fact that the mask with which he was asked to 'blindfold' himself was smeared with make-up. With considerable ingenuity, the *Sunday Express* discovered that the mask had been worn by Mr. Monkhouse the previous week and, by linking up this incident with one or two alleged exchanges between him and Gilbert, another 'feud' was born.

But the feud with the least reality of all behind it was the enmity which was supposed to exist between Gilbert and Eamonn Andrews. So strongly was this theory held by the public that I imagine it has not been killed even by the fact that Eamonn was the only man outside Gilbert's family and household to attend the private funeral service though no one knew of his intention beforehand. Gilbert always had a great affection and respect for Eamonn. Often when in doubt he would say: 'I just can't make up my mind. I won't think about it any more just now. I'll have a word with Eamonn.' It would, I think, be quite impossible to have disliked a man who appeared to me to be the most naturally charming and completely sincere of all so-called celebrities. Although we often spoke on the telephone, I met Mr. Andrews only five or six times in as many years, but on each occasion he unhesitatingly remembered not only who I was but my name too, even when Gilbert was not present to make it fairly obvious.

By the time Gilbert returned from Jamaica I had looked at dozens of flats and had whittled the long list to four or five possibles. These we now inspected together. Three were eliminated by the exorbitant price asked for furniture and fittings and a fourth because it was too gloomy. The last one we saw was, Gilbert said, exactly what he wanted. It was in a quiet Bayswater road and the outgoing tenant, an American woman, was charming. She, too, wanted quite a lot of money for the few curtains and carpets she intended to leave for the new tenant but both Gilbert and I felt we could come to a friendly agreement because she seemed in a hurry to settle the lease and return to the States. Most of her belongings, as we could see for ourselves, were crated ready to go.

She agreed to discuss the question with Gilbert's solicitor and the meeting was arranged. We waited impatiently to hear that the lease was ready for signature. Gilbert's enthusiasm had been a little sapped when the solicitor had told him that the street where he wanted to live was well known as a haunt of prostitutes. However, it wasn't the ladies of the town who finally prevented him from signing the lease, but the quite accidental discovery by Gilbert's solicitor that the American tenant had seemingly been packed and ready to leave for the States for at least six months. The sub-lease she was offering was at a rent four times what she herself paid the landlord and the 'pure wool Indian' carpets she hoped to sell were cheap cotton imitations bought specially for the purpose of making a quick and handsome profit.

More weeks of fruitless searching had passed when we saw a flat in a quiet, converted house in a South Kensington Square. It was almost ideal. It overlooked a pleasant garden, it had six large, light rooms, two luxurious bathrooms and a splendidly appointed kitchen. The outgoing tenant did not wish to sell any furnishings and though the rent was high, it was still reasonable, and the lease could be settled in a few weeks. Within a few minutes of walking into the flat Gilbert announced that he would take it, and when he learned that the outgoing tenant was the heir of a famous baron, his pleasure was noticeably increased. Unfortunately, the landlord was taken suddenly and seriously ill and for nearly a month he could not be troubled with business matters. So we had to wait, but we were so sure that all would be well, that the advice of decorators was sought, measurements for curtains and carpets were taken and we constantly discussed paint, wallpaper and materials.

Then came the blow. The landlord, recovering, had seen the name 'Gilbert Harding' on the proposed lease and, as I have told earlier, when he realized it was the same man whose name was so often splashed in the headlines, refused to let the flat to him, for fear of rowdy parties on the premises. Which was, in fact, grossly unfair. Gilbert's friends were never raucous or rowdy and neither was he. But, since there was no means of proving that, he was bitterly disappointed to lose what was to him already his new home.

But for me it came as a release. While we had been flat-hunting, in every apartment we inspected, Gilbert selected 'your room' and, supposing him to mean the office, I was cheered to find it was usually one of the nicer rooms in the flat. It wasn't until he announced that the chosen room in the South Kensington flat would be decorated and furnished to my own taste that I realized he was taking it for granted that I would live in.

At that time I lived with my sister and her family in south London. They had two young children and only three bedrooms and I had mentioned to Gilbert, in passing, that as soon as the children were old enough to need separate rooms I would have to find somewhere else to live. But the last thing I had wished or contemplated was to become part of the Harding household. I knew that, if I did so, I would lose my freedom, for Gilbert demanded companionship constantly and he would expect me to be always available to give it.

I enjoy seeing 'high life' and living in luxury as much as the next man, but I well knew that I had not the stamina to be both secretary and companion: to work all day, I needed to get to bed at a reasonable hour, while Gilbert could, and often did, stay up until dawn several nights in succession. Nor did I feel equal to devoting myself to his mental and emotional demands for eighteen hours a day: I had my own friends and relations to whom I was strongly attached.

Already I had had several evenings out with him and each one of them had left me feeling exhausted for several days. We had celebrated his recovery from illness by going to the theatre. But ten minutes after the curtain rose I became aware of the rumblings beside me . . . 'Piffle . . . rubbish . . . mouthing mummery . . . Come on, we're going. I can't stand any more.' I followed him out and into the cocktail bar of a near-by hotel. There was a row of empty stools at the bar but the one Gilbert arbitrarily chose was occupied by a briefcase. Its owner sat on the next stool and he at once put out a hand to move it. Inexplicably this infuriated Gilbert and the astonished customer was overwhelmed with insult. The manager's urgent tact was wasted and once more I followed Gilbert out – but not before, without in the least relenting, he had managed to order and swallow two large whiskies.

I had previously booked a table for supper at a luxurious restaurant. We went straight there and, of course, arrived at least two hours before the appointed time so that the manager had to ask us to wait awhile. Once more Gilbert began loudly to rumble and grumble until, after feeding the fire of his complaint with more whisky at the bar, he left – 'and believe me, sir, I could not be in a happier frame of mind. Leaving your squalid café gives me infinitely greater pleasure than I ever had on entering it' – while I followed. Three or four drinks taken on an empty stomach affect me quickly and I was by then in such a state of embarrassment and despair that only two courses appeared possible – I could leave at once and go home to bed or accept some kind of anaesthesia in alcohol. Somehow, one could not leave Gilbert to endure such a mood alone, so I chose the second course.

From the restaurant we went to one night-club after another. In each of them a wholly unnecessary scene was staged. At last, at about two in the morning, we sat down to the promised quiet supper. As each dish was brought, Gilbert found fault with it and it was whisked away before I had time to try a mouthful. Finally I found courage to complain that I was very hungry and had reached the stage when even cold mutton stew would be welcome. Inevitably, his fury turned on me. For the consideration of all the customers, he offered in a booming voice a list of my shortcomings as a private secretary, stinting neither their curiosity nor his imagination. 'And so,' he concluded, as his invective began to fail, 'it must be obvious to even your warped and moronic intellect that I can no longer retain your services.'

The act was over. The whole restaurant was silent as he raised a finger to the waiter, signed the bill, over-tipped everyone in sight and stalked up the stairs. I was abandoned, at three o'clock in the morning, in London's smartest night-club. Even today I am still awed by the resource I brought to the situation. Gathering such dignity as a publicly sacked secretary could hope to retain, I walked to the telephone, ordered a car from the firm Gilbert always used and was driven the twelve miles home at his expense.

When I arrived at Cadogan Place next morning, a Saturday, beginning to savour the relief of looking for more placid occupation, Mrs. Clarke told me that Mr. Harding had come home little more than an hour earlier and was asleep in bed. As I passed his open bedroom door and looked warily in, he sat bolt upright, glaring at me.

'How is it,' he asked sorrowfully, 'than one can never take you out for a quiet and pleasant evening without your making an unpleasant and embarrassing scene?'

He sank back on the pillows and, when I left three hours later, he was still sleeping peacefully. On the Monday morning it was obvious that I was forgiven for my shameful lapse, for I was greeted with the usual grumbles about the burden of work ahead of us.

The near-miss of the South Kensington flat drove me to decide that I must at once find a flat of my own and so began a double search. I won, finding a flat north of Oxford Street only a week or two before the final approval of Gilbert's new London home in Weymouth Street, less than five minutes' walk away. It was a great relief and happiness to Gilbert to have found at last 'a place of his own'; it gave him a new, if transient, security. And it had been a rather hectic search in the last few weeks, for he had been immensely busy – apart from his weekly articles for *The People* and *Picture Post*, there had been engagements all over the country and performances in a series of advertising films for Players' cigarettes. One of his jobs at that time had moved him very deeply – a lecture on his career in radio and television to the prisoners at Wormwood Scrubs. 'Can there be anything more terrible than the complete deprivation of liberty?' he said on his return. 'I cannot remember ever having spoken to a more attentive and receptive audience. It made me feel desperately humble.' A newspaper report said that he had addressed every prisoner he spoke to as 'sir' and he had told them that, during his war-time work with the B B C, 'we lived in conditions of security almost equalling yours'.

And he had had another incident in the headlines. On the Saturday evening of Whit week-end, he had been bitterly attacked by a woman who mistook him for Raymond Glendenning, whose commentary on the Derby had grossly disappointed many punters. Gilbert defended himself hotly and, no doubt, impolitely, and an abrupt defensive movement from the woman caught his elbow and jerked his glass so sharply as to cut his face. The wound was insignificant, but somehow all concerned found themselves at the local police station. Gilbert protested the whole incident was forgotten already, he was not prepared to bring any charge against the unfortunate woman. But already the newspapermen were alerted and the reporters were telephoning the flat. The incident, with statements from both parties, made the front page for several days and the *Evening Standard* published a cartoon showing several men on an Underground escalator, each of them bearing some resemblance to Mr. Harding, some to Mr. Glendenning. And each of them wore a cross of sticking-plaster on his chin.

It was at about this time, however, that he found a new delight. *Guys and Dolls* was playing at the Coliseum and it enchanted Gilbert. Not only did he go to see it again and again but bought tickets for his friends so that they might share his pleasure. He knew so well how to make a success of such a gift. He took a box for Kate Wadleigh, for instance, and booked for her a table for four for supper, telephoning himself to the manager to encourage him to give the party everything of the very best. Then, on his way from one engagement to another, he dropped in at the theatre and, during the interval, called on Mrs. Wadleigh and her friends in the box to make sure they were enjoying themselves. That kind of gesture was typical of him in those days. When he couldn't manage to entertain his friends himself, he took pleasure in giving them a luxurious evening out at his expense. And somehow he always made them feel that they would only please him by eating and drinking as well as he would have done himself.

His generosity could be practical, too. At that time his income was only about half of what it was to become a few years later but he was less cautious about giving. A man employed by one of the car-hire firms he used had driven him on several long journeys and happened to mention that, though he was trying to buy a house on mortgage, he was short of the deposit by something over a hundred pounds. Within a few days, Gilbert had found the money for him. A friend needed a loan of three hundred pounds to put his business on its feet again, another had pressing debts: the money was soon found. One evening another friend called in great distress. Money he had been expecting, he said, had failed to come through and tradesmen had told his wife that until the bills were settled she could have no further supplies. Gilbert wanted to help, but he had no more than about five pounds on him and the banks were closed. Then he remembered the Dimple Haig whisky bottle into which he dropped the sixpences from his change each night. He asked me to go to the bedroom, empty the bottle into an envelope and bring it to him. 'I think I can manage the £20, after all,' he told his friend, 'if you don't mind most of it in sixpences.' But the offer was turned down with fury. 'How can my wife possibly humiliate herself – and me – by paying the milkman and the grocer with sixpences?'

Much to Gilbert's sorrow this same man, a few months later, in a drunken temper, deliberately smashed a lovely crystal goblet. Gilbert had often told me that he had in his youth learned not to become too jealous of his possessions. But this goblet was an exception. It had originally been given by the Queen Mother to the Hostel of God for the Dying when she opened a new wing built with money which Gilbert had helped to raise. In their turn the authorities there had presented it to Gilbert in recognition of his part.

But possessions became temporarily important when we moved into the new flat at Weymouth Street. Furniture which had been in store for some time – from the Twickenham flat and the Hereford house – was now to be delivered to the flat, but with only two rooms yet decorated and the painters still hard at work we agreed it should, as far as possible, be piled into one room for sorting. Even Gilbert did not know quite what, or how much, to expect. To the despair – and delay – of the decorators, we finally had three rooms stacked to the ceiling with assorted beds, chairs, tables, and carpets. On the day we took possession, an old friend from the Bradford days called at Cadogan Place just as the furniture van was leaving. It was Joan Smith. Whenever she passed through London she had always telephoned or called on Gilbert. On this occasion she was even more welcome than usual, for she came with us in the taxi to Weymouth Street, borrowed a large overall from our new 'daily', and buckled down to the job of unpacking crates of china and glass. Luckily Gilbert, never a willing or dexterous manual worker, had a radio engagement that morning and we let him go with a sigh of relief. We were both grubby and dishevelled when he telephoned about noon to suggest that we 'come and have a proper lunch at the Ivy. If you don't, you'll just make a cup of coffee and a bit of bread and cheese and neither of you will eat properly. I'll see you there at one sharp!' He rang off before I had time to point out that we were in no condition to lunch at a smart West End restaurant. We washed and brushed and hurried off to meet him, to be fussed over and fed with delicacies as though we were Olympic heroes instead of rather drab and exhausted manual labourers. But we managed to stifle his desire to linger over the coffee and rushed back to get at least the kitchen and Gilbert's bedroom into a passable condition for that night.

It was certainly because of the happy relationship we established that day that, when Joan Smith became Gilbert's housekeeper in Brighton, we were already firm friends.

Gilbert found a great deal of happiness from the idea of this home. The wallpaper in the hall – ivy leaves clambering on a white ground – the musical chimes of the doorbell, the row of whisks and strainers and ladles hanging below the mantelshelf in the wonderfully appointed kitchen, the strangely mixed choice of pictures in the drawing-room, were an endless source of question and comment for his visitors. Where, at Cadogan Place, he had apologized for his surroundings, now he modestly offered his own highly individual taste for commendation.

It was at this time that the whole problem of Independent Television became important. It had only been in existence for a short time and there were rumours of the lavish money that might soon be made by those who accepted contracts with I T V. Warily the B B C approached some of their stars with the offer of a long-term exclusive contract, and Gilbert was delighted with the terms they offered. He was on the verge of accepting when an agent of one of the independent companies approached him with the offer of a contract worth not only several times what the B B C suggested but more than twice his total income at that time. But Gilbert, as was later revealed in the *Face to Face* programme and even in the memorial programme after his death, though a rebel, was no adventurer. He needed security. After long discussions and arguments he eventually signed, with relief, the B B C contract for a three-year term. It guaranteed him a minimum of £7,000 a year.

At this time, apart from his weekly columns for Odham's Press, much of Gilbert's earnings came from publicity work – appearances at the opening of department stores and exhibitions, advertisements for such varied products as ball-point pens, alarm clocks, and television insurance. He also took part in documentary films and, occasionally, ordinary feature films. It was some years later that he signed a contract to advertise exclusively Maclean's indigestion remedies, which brought him a considerable income. This particular contract worried him greatly. He did, quite genuinely, believe in the product he advertised. He really did carry tablets in his pocket. But he always felt that the money was much too easily earned and was shamed by 'the exorbitant value of my unprepossessing features'.

One of the publicity stories he agreed to at this time was an article about the kitchen at Weymouth Street, and his photograph was taken, at the cooker, swathed in an apron. It was a very true picture. He really let himself go in that kitchen. It was a fairly big one – and it needed to be, because Gilbert was not only a very untidy cook but needed many underlings to cope with the more menial tasks. His culinary imagination outstripped his capacity for hard work. When he invited friends to lunch he often planned over-elaborate menus which entailed three or four of us racing around while he sat, like a modern Mrs. Beaton, saying, 'Pass me six eggs . . . and a bowl . . . no, no, you cretin, I mean a saucepan . . . and a glass of brandy . . .' until the guests arrived, when he would sit happily dispensing drinks while I took over the role of chef. I became an exceedingly competent cook while I was Gilbert Harding's secretary! He, of course, gloried in his new role of host in his own home.

This was, perhaps, one of the most settled and satisfying periods of Gilbert Harding's public life. It was a stage at which he was accepted in the press as 'a warm, friendly Harding, of which we don't see enough', in the *Daily Mirror*, while Beverley Baxter wrote in the *Evening Standard* that 'if Gilbert Harding sneezes, it is news. If he is rude, or if he is polite, it is news. If he is ill, or if he is well, it is news.' The literary editor of the *Sunday Times* said the same thing to me in a different way: 'The day is not far distant when even Gilbert's belches will be news.'

It was news, too, when he introduced Marlene Dietrich at the Café de Paris, where she was appearing in cabaret. Noël Coward introduced her the first night, Robert Morley the second – and Gilbert the third. As the time approached he became jittery. He had always deeply admired Miss Dietrich, but he had never met her. So, before he could introduce her to the audience, he had himself to be introduced to her. He was discreetly called from his table alongside the dance floor to be conducted to her dressing-room for the first meeting. Five minutes later he returned. 'Never in my life,' he said, his eyes gleaming, 'have I ever met a more beautiful and desirable woman!' His hands were still shaking as he rose to meet the star in the spotlight where she suddenly appeared to the audience, and his admiration was patent. The cheers that echoed his greeting as he kissed Marlene's hand were doubled when she bent down to kiss his cheek. They became great friends, for he must have been in the audience more than a dozen nights during the three weeks she appeared there and several times sent flowers to her dressing-room. Before she returned to the States she gave Gilbert an affectionately inscribed photograph and a note thanking him for his friendship.

CHAPTER EIGHT

PUBLIC FACE

A THING which both my employer and I found puzzling was that, whenever he was indiscreet, a newspaper reporter just happened to be around to overhear it. This was so when he returned from a brief holiday of about ten days in Belgium and Luxembourg in 1954. He had stayed a few days at Ostend where the Belgian Tourist Board, not unnaturally hoping for valuable publicity, insisted that he should be their guest. He was expected to sample the treatment of the town's thermal establishment, but he enjoyed neither the mineral waters he was expected to drink nor the strenuous pummelling of athletic masseurs. The weather was bad and, wherever he went, even in the remotest country districts, he was beseiged by British holiday-makers clamouring for his autograph. Even the return trip was exasperating, for he was separated from his luggage, which travelled on another boat, and there was some confusion about his cabin reservation. No doubt he was tetchy when he finally arrived at Dover and next day the *Daily Sketch* carried the headline 'Harding says: I'm Cured of Travel' over a report in which he was quoted as saying, 'Oh, the chaos and the horror of it. I would rather swim the Channel next time.'

A few weeks later Gilbert took another short holiday, spending a long weekend with his valued friend Lord Beaverbrook at his villa at Cap d'Ail in the south of France. Even this brief relaxation had its trials, for the plane on which he should have travelled from Nice to London late one evening developed a fault and the flight was postponed until the following morning. I knew nothing of this and was surprised to find the flat empty when I got to Weymouth Street at the appointed time. Almost immediately, the telephone rang. It was Gilbert, furious, ringing from London airport.

'How *could* you keep me standing in this stuffy box? What on earth were you doing? Where has this car come from? Who sent it?'

I just yammered. He banged down the receiver before I had time to ask what he was talking about. It appeared later that, unable to reach me by telephone the evening before, Gilbert had telephoned the BBC and asked them to cancel the car due to collect him that evening at the airport, and to arrange for it to come the next morning. But Gilbert's usual firm could not take the morning booking and so the BBC official had laid on a different firm. Already furious about the night's delay, Gilbert had refused to get into the car until he had discovered who had sent it to meet him. However, having got rid of his anger on me, he quietly entered the car and was driven to London. I discovered what had happened and rang back to the airport, but by that time he was on his way.

This did not set my mind at rest. Soon after his departure for France, I had realized that I had forgotten to pack pyjamas in his case. I had been waiting to be told of this omission ever since, and when I heard his key in the lock, my inside twisted into knots. As I had expected, he stormed in, exclaiming about the way he had been treated. When he had denounced me for the fourth time, and each time in finely-flowing but quite different phrases, I took advantage of a pause to point out that I had learned only just before his telephone call that he had not returned the previous evening as arranged. There was a short silence. Then:

'My dear Podge,' he said, with an irresistible smile of humility and apology, 'I am not only an unmitigated fool but I am a stupendously stupid and selfish boor. How furiously you must hate me. Honestly, I cannot conceive how you can bear with me. At times like this I can't bear myself.' And so the pyjamas were never mentioned.

As a rule a delayed flight merits no more than three lines in the evening papers, but somehow, several newspapers had discovered that Gilbert was having to spend an unexpected night in Nice and reporters had telephoned him there to get his reactions. They had not been disappointed. Next morning the papers carried quotes from him, like, 'Nice is anything but nice', 'I've just had dinner at unimaginable cost', and 'The people here are frightful'. His morning temper was, almost certainly, caused by remorse for his own indiscretions.

Remorse was the feeling that haunted Gilbert almost daily. 'Showing off' seemed to be a compulsion with him, even when it was quite unnecessary. When he was a small boy at the spartan Royal Orphanage at Wolverhampton, the headmaster had told his mother, 'Gilbert has an unfortunate tendency to show off.' But it was a tendency based on timidity, not on over-confidence. A stutterer in childhood, a promising scholar who had achieved only a Third at Cambridge, Gilbert was dogged, I felt, by the belief that his character was not as great, nor his ability as high as others supposed, so he tried to assume the personality expected of him. With a less sensitive man, it might have succeeded, but Gilbert was too astute to be taken in by his own characterizations and, when he realized how far he had fallen short, he was ashamed.

That summer, two public occasions brought out this unhappy condition. In September he went to Blackpool to press the official switch that lit up the Blackpool illuminations and, later, made a good-will visit to Grimsby, organized by the White Fish Authority. He was well paid for both trips and they both brought 'disfiguring' press publicity.

He had walked out of the Grimsby luncheon. 'Clash Over *Sauce à la Harding*' . . . 'He Broke Up The Lunch Party' . . . 'Fish Isn't Gilbert's Dish,' said the headlines. His own account to me was hazy. 'It's so wrong to have any kind of sauce with fried fish . . . and to give it my name!' It appeared, from the newspaper accounts, that at first the visit had gone according to plan. Gilbert had toured the docks 'as placid as a plaice', said the *Daily Mail*. Then came the official luncheon – with fried Dover sole and fried potatoes and a special sauce *à la Harding*. No doubt the friendly fishermen had given him plenty of gin as an aperitif, but they had aroused two of his most rooted prejudices. He considered fish and chips to be a splendid native dish, with no need for embellishments, and he loathed Frenchified menus. So he refused to make his prepared speech and, when he had eaten – having forced the Mayor, the Town Clerk and twenty-five leading trawler-owners to eat their fish and chips according to his own taste – he left the party.

Blackpool's illuminations had long been switched off for the winter when that particular storm broke. It was a Council discussion which revealed his sins. The fee for his appearance had been fifty pounds. To earn it, Gilbert had to travel north, meet the Corporation officials, publicly turn a switch and, he had supposed, get to bed in reasonable time to catch an early train back in the morning. But after the official turning on of the lights, he had been taken on a coach-tour of the town with members of the Corporation and Council, arriving at the Imperial Hotel, where a room had been booked for him, at eleven o'clock. What he had not reckoned with was that his show-business friends and acquaintances, in Blackpool for the summer season, would then arrive to greet him. As if by magic drinks appeared, and it was after three o'clock in the morning before the final 'Good night, Gilbert' was said. In the morning, when he asked for his bill, the reply was, 'The Corporation have asked us to send it to them, Mr. Harding.' And, as far as he was concerned, that was that.

But the committees of the Corporation of Blackpool, though having steeled themselves to pay a fee and bed and breakfast terms, jibbed at entertainment expenses. The Council referred back the hotel bill and decided that it should be reconsidered at the next meeting. They did not suggest that Mr. Harding should pay it himself. They did not communicate with him on the matter, But, of course, when the inevitable newspaper stories appeared, the impression was that Gilbert had given a party at the Corporation's expense. Immediately, he telephoned the Town Clerk and asked if he might settle the bill. The Town Clerk was shocked that Mr. Harding should have been disturbed by the publicity and would not hear of such a thing. The subject was kept alive by the press, however, until the next Council meeting when it was reported that 'a mystery man, whose name officials refused to reveal' had paid all but £2 13s. 4d. of the bill. The committee quickly decided to pay the balance. The strange report was never officially confirmed and Gilbert never found out who had paid the money he would so gladly have given himself.

Probably the only way in which Gilbert could justify his notoriety was to turn it to useful account in the cause of charity. At this time he was invited, together with the late Marquis and the Marchioness of Carisbrooke, to be patron of a special performance of the play *Bell, Book and Candle* in aid of an old people's housing charity. While he sat with Lord and Lady Carisbrooke and Mrs. Barbara Back in a box, he had nevertheless insisted that I should attend and I had a seat at the end of the front row of the dress circle and an invitation to share champagne and sandwiches in the ante-room during the interval. As I settled comfortably into my seat, an attendant whispered a message. Mr. Harding was obliged to attend a press conference during the interval: would I be kind enough to act as host in his stead?

I cannot remember a word or a gesture of that first act. I shivered with terror at the thought of standing-in for one who had always seemed to me the perfect host. I nerved myself to enter the ante-room and, almost immediately, silently cursed the earlier decision that the room was too small to permit of waiters: I had not only to welcome the guests, but also to open the champagne. The first cork refused to be withdrawn but, seeing my struggles, Lord Carisbrooke insisted on holding the bottle while I tugged. The other bottles yielded more easily but I was very grateful to a young man who had covered up my struggles by handing round the sand-wiches. I already knew some of the guests – Rex Harrison, the star of the play, Mary Malcolm and her (then) husband, Sir Basil Bart-lett, her mother Lady Malcolm, Lord and Lady Carisbrooke and Barbara Back. It was not until a few seconds before the end of the interval that I was introduced to the other guests. The young man who had handed round the sandwiches was Dominic Elwes, whose runaway marriage some time later was splashed in the headlines for many weeks.

Mainly I accepted the reflected glory of being 'Gilbert Harding's secretary', and tried to be unobtrusive when famous names were part of his working life. The exception was Gracie Fields. For busi-ness reasons I was in touch with her manager, Mrs. Bert Aza, when I managed to pluck up courage to ask if I personally, Roger Storey, could perhaps meet her. I had been her ardent worshipper since the age of eight or nine and I can still truthfully say that no one has ever taken her place in my admiration and affection. So, when a few weeks later Gracie came to London, I was invited to meet her in her dressing-room after a Sunday night concert at the Gau-mont State Theatre, Kilburn. Though I was in daily contact with a star almost as famous as she, I knew I should be so overwhelmed with excitement that I would forget every word Gracie said im-mediately afterwards. So I asked if I might take a friend along. Only one other person was present – her husband, Boris Alperovici – and while Gracie brushed her hair and repaired her make-up, she talked, and made us talk, as naturally and unaffectedly as if we had been sitting over a cup of tea in a kitchen in Rochdale. She spoke very warmly of Gilbert and of his performances and the ten or fifteen minutes I spent there seemed to come to an end in as many seconds. A few weeks later, she and Gilbert were fellow-guests at an enormous party at Claridge's, given by Sir Bernard and Lady Docker, and my day – my year – was made when I got to work the next morning. Gilbert was still in bed when I arrived but as I passed his bedroom door, he called out:

'Can that be that delightful young man, my secretary, who is so very fond of me?'

My heart sank. I tried hard to think of something I had left undone yesterday that he might have discovered overnight. I turned reluctantly and went in to face him.

'Good morning,' I said. 'That's me. Why?'

Gilbert knew exactly what I was thinking. There was a malicious gleam in his eye as he gave me one of his most charming smiles. 'Oh, that's what Gracie Fields called you last night when she asked me to remember her to you!' And I, of course, blushed with pleasure, so that he laughed delightedly.

Sometimes those early-morning encounters with my boss were shattering. He rarely went to bed, when he was in London, before two or three in the morning because he invited friends home to share his greatest pleasure – talking. So he was often asleep when I arrived at nine-fifteen. When he was fairly fit, this did not worry him and he would wake about half-past, ready for work. But sometimes he would leave me notes. Once I had left a reminder to myself on the office table – 'Shampoo Cham-pu' – to buy dog soap. In the morning I found these words added: 'Clean poor G.H.'s tie and see to his apothecary's requirements.' And, across one corner, 'Get one's cards'. But my cards were not, when he woke up, handed to me. On another of my self-reminders – a piece of paper crammed with notes to do this, get that, telephone so-and-so, I found the words 'Love to all. And thanks. G.H.' One morning, he rolled over and opened his eyes and handed me a piece of paper. 'Remind me about these when I wake up,' he said, and fell straight asleep again. The list was: *Tongue in 'frig. General indifference and neglect. Beastliness. Ugliness. Insolence.* I put the tinned tongue in the refrigerator and prepared myself to answer the charges against me. It was nearly eleven when he came briskly into the office. I silently picked up the list and held it out. 'Yes,' he said, 'admit it, you're beastly and ugly and insolent and you neglect me shockingly.' 'No,' I firmly replied. 'Ah, well, I was afraid you wouldn't agree. Where's the morning post?'

I had the chance to meet many interesting and famous people when the BBC decided that they were not using Gilbert's talents to the full. They wanted to give him a programme that would take him out of the class of quizzes and parlour games, so they announced with a flourish of publicity a series of Gilbert Harding Interviews on the Home Service, twice a week, in which he would talk to all manner of people, some famous and others quite unknown. In order to make the programme flexible and topical, the names of his guests were not to be announced in advance.

It was hard work, not only for Gilbert, but for the producer, his friend of many years, Archie Gordon – a friend whose judgement and authority he always accepted. Very often plans would be made to interview someone when, at the very last minute, he was unable either to make a live broadcast or to pre-record an interview. When this happened only a few hours before the broadcast was due, tempers and nerves were strained to the limit. To interview Beatrice Lillie, Gilbert and Archie had to travel up to Manchester where she was appearing in revue, and be back early the next morning to record an interview with Sir Malcolm Sargent, who was about to leave for a long tour abroad. Bob Hope, when he came to London, was terribly difficult to get hold of. A bevy of secretaries, press agents, and script writers kept telephone inquiries at bay and it seemed impossible that we could ever fix a definite date. Then one night Gilbert took me to the Café de Paris to see Noël Coward's cabaret act. As we were leaving, Gilbert noticed Bob Hope and several members of his entourage at a table in the cocktail bar. He asked if we might join them for a moment and, over a drink, the interview was settled in a matter of minutes.

When people were unable to go to Broadcasting House, Gilbert and Archie took a tape-recorder to stage the interview at their home or hotel. The interview with Dr. Bustamante, Prime Minister of Jamaica, was done in that way. So was the interview with Dr. Robert Hutchins, the President of the University of Chicago. When the programme could be made at Broadcasting House, I usually went with Gilbert to the studio. My most vivid memory of such an occasion was when Peter Ustinov was the guest. He had just come back from America and he kept us so entertained with stories and imitations of some of the people he had met there, that I began to think they would never get down to the actual job of recording. But the man who made the greatest impression on me was relatively unknown. He was a missionary who had gone to India as a very young man and had founded a school for orphan boys. He was a quiet, unassuming and wholly dedicated man. As we left the studio, Gilbert said: 'That is a truly good and Christian man. I feel the better for having met him.'

For an unknown person, it was often highly embarrassing to accompany Gilbert in public, for his fans seemed to be everywhere, and he seldom went unrecognized. Very often, on seeing Gilbert, people would stop dead in their tracks, mouths agape. Many would rush up to him and insist on shaking his hand or, if he were in a bar, buying him a drink, which he always tried to refuse. One type I dreaded meeting was the 'I must touch you' type. They seemed unable to believe he was real until they had made physical contact. Gilbert always hated to be touched unnecessarily and such incidents always made him furious. Walking through Covent Garden to *The People* office, past vegetable warehouses and lorries, he would try to keep a grin of good fellowship on his face as he endured shouts of 'What's *my* line, Gilbert?' or 'How's your indigestion, Gilbert?' One day, as he left *The People* offices to keep a luncheon engagement, Kate Wadleigh was with him. 'Don't leave me till I find a cab,' he begged, 'then perhaps no one will come up and speak to me.' They stood in apparently earnest conversation for a moment or two until a taxi arrived. As he opened the door, Gilbert bent down and gratefully kissed her on the cheek. Such a vast Cockney cheer went up from the market porters that Kate felt herself blushing to the soles of her feet.

Worst of all were the autograph hunters. They were ubiquitous and merciless. In the streets, in trains, in restaurants, they crowded round him with programmes or bits of paper or menus to be signed. If he claimed that he had no pen and could not sign, there was usually someone to say, 'Well, you *ought* to have one.' Once when I was with him, he was even asked, to his intense disgust, to sign his name on a still damp and sticky ice-cream wrapper. When he declined, the mother of the child who had asked used language that no lady should ever have heard, let alone used. Sometimes such people would discuss me – 'Who's he? Is he on television?' The answers varied from 'Course, that's Richard Attenborough', to 'Of course, I've seen him, but I can't remember the name', or the curt, damning 'Nobody'.

Once I was travelling back by train from Hereford with Gilbert, when the train stopped in some station for several minutes. He was sound asleep and I was reading, but a low murmur of voices made me look up. There, with their noses squashed against the glass, or standing on tiptoe to look over others' shoulders were about twenty people. They were discussing us, pointing, grinning, waving. I felt like an octopus in an aquarium. What to do? Should I look away and seem snooty; should I wave and appear presumptuous; or should I continue to sit there and look a fool? I chose the last course and then, as the train began to move, grinned at them in a wild and lunatic fashion. If such public interest made me, who was not its object, squirm, what torment it must have been for the man, so basically lonely and insecure, at whom it was aimed.

In the autumn of 1954, when *What's My Line?* started again, Gilbert was tired and far from well. For the first few weeks his behaviour on the panel, though not outrageous enough to make the headlines, was irritable and sometimes ungracious. In one performance early in December, his temper was frayed from the start. His first victim was a carpet designer whom he treated with contempt because he could not decide if his calling were artistic. He protested volubly when Eamonn Andrews, in order to avoid the programme overrunning its allotted span, put a time limit on the questioning. He crossed verbal swords with another challenger, an exhibition organizer who, before his occupation was guessed, had said his job was nothing to do with trade. Finally, as the last challenger signed-in, Eamonn announced that there was only one minute before the end of the programme and Gilbert burst into an attack on the BBC's new policy of fading-out programmes which were overrunning. None of this was particularly scandalous, but the newspapers had left Gilbert alone lately and so they rushed in to print the story. They had even more to tell when it was announced a few days later that he was to be given three weeks' rest from *What's My Line?* 'Aha!' said the newspapers. 'Aha!' grinned the gossip-loving public. But they were wrong in believing the BBC had suspended him. In fact, Gilbert had been pressing for some time for a rest. This time, when he renewed his request, it was granted. But three weeks was not enough. He returned to the programme, still tired, still feeling unwell, and at length, after close friends and I had constantly urged it, he consulted his doctor. The doctor in turn pressed him to see a specialist. The specialist sent him to a great consultant, Lord Horder. It was he who first discovered signs of heart disorder and he advised Gilbert that his only chance of making a complete recovery was to take a long, complete and immediate rest.

So barely had he returned to *What's My Line?*, when every daily newspaper announced that Gilbert's appearance on the programme at the end of the week would be the last public engagement of any kind that he would fulfil for at least three months. The following day he would begin a course of intensive treatment and dieting.

For Gilbert the outlook was abysmally dreary. For me it was terrifying. He had persuaded his doctors that he would respond more quickly to treatment at home than in hospital and the prospect of having my boss at home and theoretically in bed for three months made me sick with nervousness.

Tongue in frig
general indifference
+ neglect—
beastliness &
ugliness
insolence—

THE NOTE GILBERT LEFT FOR ME

CHAPTER NINE

DIETICIAN'S DESPAIR

IF you are unable to tell a lie, you should never accept the post of private secretary to a public figure.

I was paid to be a barrier between my employer and anything that might worry, inconvenience or discomfort him. Which meant that if his doctors imposed on him conditions he did not wish to fulfil, then it was my duty to cover up his lapses. Yet, against his profoundest wish, my more urgent duty was to keep him happy, alive and well. That meant, on innumerable occasions, subtlety of which I hardly felt capable. While telling a thumping lie, I had to try to imply that the truth I was hiding was not quite so bad as might be suspected. This was the position I found myself in with Lord Horder.

Impressed by the fact that he could take no higher advice than that of one of the Queen's doctors, Gilbert tried hard at first to follow the prescribed régime. He stayed in bed until lunch-time each day and from then, until about ten o'clock in the evening, he sat around in nightshirt (a new and comforting fad) and dressing-gown, watching television, reading, or directing my efforts to make his meagre permitted meals more interesting and tasty. At that stage he seemed happy to realize that no demands of any kind could be made upon him. But it did not take him very long sub-consciously to appreciate that if there were no demands on his sympathy or his attention, it might be that they were unwanted. He also, like so many people with no self-love, became intensely bored with his own company.

So he lifted, peremptorily, the restriction on visitors. Lord Horder allowed him two callers each day, for half an hour each. Within a few days, his visitors arrived five or six at a time and had to be given hospitality. According to his strict diet, Gilbert was allowed half a bottle of light wine each day, but spirits had to be produced for his friends when they called and no one could stop Gilbert joining in. Far too often, faced with the carefully-measured allowance of fats and starch, he would demand 'just another half slice of bread' or 'a little bit more butter. Were you brought up in the workhouse, too, that you learned to spread it so thinly?' More than once he dressed and announced his intention of going out to a restaurant or to his club, but by reminding him of the foul weather outside and the flood of publicity that would follow a public appearance, I managed to persuade him to stay at home.

I had been extremely nervous of my first meeting with Lord Horder. It was always essential that there should be a close liaison between myself and Gilbert's doctors because at that time it was only I who could carry out their instructions or make a report on the patient's progress, and I wondered how a famous specialist would deal with me. I need have had no fears. He was a small, friendly man, not in the least pompous, with a delightful sense of humour and I soon found it natural to talk to him freely. Whenever he called on Gilbert, he pretended to treat me as a fellow-doctor and I still have the letter which he sent to thank me for a cheese I brought him from Wensleydale some weeks after Gilbert's recovery. After hoping that 'our patient continues to make good progress', he signed the letter 'Your sincere colleague, Horder.'

But Lord Horder was not happy about his patient. He was much too wise not to know that Gilbert was ignoring many of his recommendations and, at each visit, he questioned me closely about Gilbert's health and behaviour since his last call. It was just as impossible for me to tell Lord Horder the whole truth as it was to make Gilbert follow his orders. I felt that if I confirmed the doctor's suspicions he would probably, and justifiably, withdraw from the case. For many weeks my conscience, my sympathies and my loyalties were all highly strained. It was a relief, therefore, when Lord Horder arrived one day to find Gilbert holding what amounted to a small party. There were at least five visitors; champagne and spirits were flowing freely and Gilbert was holding a tumblerful of whisky and soda.

The next day Gilbert received a solemn letter from Lord Horder. It said that Mr. Harding could hope for no improvement in his condition unless he tried very much harder to follow the régime which had been recommended. It pointed out that, if Mr. Harding was unable to make the necessary effort, it seemed pointless to waste his money and Lord Horder's time in continuing the treatment. A rebuke, even when as mildly-phrased as this, was something Gilbert could never accept. He dictated an immediate reply in grieved and rather offensive terms. 'There now, how about that?' he said, flinging the letter across to me. 'If you are asking me what I think of your reply, Mr. Harding,' I said, 'to my mind it is unwise, unkind and ungrateful.' For a few seconds I expected him to have a heart attack and collapse. Then his face changed completely.

'My dear Podge, my good counsellor,' he said quietly, 'you are absolutely right. Moreover, I didn't mean a word of it. I was deliberately working myself up into a fury to stop myself feeling ashamed. I have been doing that much, much too often these last few weeks and you have borne the brunt of it, poor Roger. But I *do* feel ashamed and I had better confess it. Let me dictate a different answer.' He did. And this time it was a charming note of apology and a promise to make a greater effort to do as he was told. For several days he stuck rigorously to his diet, drank no spirits at all and allowed only one visitor a day to call on him.

A few days after that letter, Lord Horder's secretary telephoned to ask me to call at his consulting-rooms that afternoon. I was distressed when I saw him. He seemed, perhaps because he was very tired, to have aged considerably in the past few days. He spoke quite frankly and told me he was extremely worried and dissatisfied with Gilbert's progress. 'There is no doubt that he will recover sufficiently to resume his normal life, but his recovery will be far from complete. And it may not be for long.' He was shocked by his patient's refusal, or inability, to co-operate wholeheartedly and felt that he himself was much to blame for not having insisted from the beginning that Gilbert should be treated in a nursing home. I did my utmost to try to convince him that I knew, from experience, that Gilbert would never have agreed to such a suggestion.

I deliberately walked as slowly as possible back to Weymouth Street, for I wanted to decide just how much I could tell Gilbert of my conversation with Lord Horder. I knew that he would ask for a verbatim report and this, I felt, I could not possibly give. But the little I could tell him would take only a few minutes and

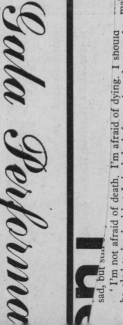

Gala Performance

'Why treat good music as sacred? Why not *enjoy* it? Let's knock out the pomposity and have fun.' So says

8.10 Richard Attenborough, and the sentiment is shared by two friends of his—Malcolm Arnold, conductor and composer, and Julian Bream, guitarist. Together the three form a resident team talking about the music and introducing the stars in *Gala Performance*. Starting tonight, this new series will have the world's finest artists—singers, dancers, pianists, and other instrumentalists—bringing you the best-loved classics in an easy, relaxed setting.

Gala Performance opens with a welcome for

sad, but sure...

'I'm not afraid of death, I'm afraid of dying. I should be glad to be dead but I don't look forward to the actual process of dying.' (*Gilbert Harding*)

'He was a wonderful friend and a kind man whose public image was his private misfortune.' (*Tom Sloan*)

'I've often thought I'd like to join a monastery but then I'd have to behave myself much more than I'm able to do.' (*Gilbert Harding*)

...making, cruelty. The world is a duller place without this vehement, vulnerable man.' (*Kenneth Adam*)

I never knew an unhappier man. I never knew a man who was more determined to be his own worst enemy. I never knew a man who was so easily or so sorely tried. And I never knew a man who more effortlessly inspired love, loyalty, and friendship.

nd **Rudolf Nureyev**. They'll be seen first in a pas de deux from the glamorously oriental Gayaneh suite by the Russian composer Khachaturyan, then in the famous pas de deux from Act II of Swan Lake. Another guest is the brilliant Hungarian pianist **György Cziffra**, playing Chopin's tempestuous Polonaise No. 6 and the dazzling, fantastically-difficult Grand Galop Chromatique by Liszt. That favourite Australian soprano, **Joan Hammond**, springs a surprise with an aria from the opera Clari, or the Maid of Milan. The aria? None other than 'Home, Sweet Home,' which topped the pops, so to speak, in 1825.

Four years ago Malcolm Arnold, who tonight also conducts the **Philharmonia Orchestra**, wrote a guitar concerto specially for Julian Bream, and the two will join forces in the final movement. Despite his work for serious guitar music, London-born Julian Bream is no 'square'; he likes jazz, which matches up with the broad aims of Gala Performance. 'We're ready to try anything good of its kind,' says **Patricia Foy**, the producer.

ERNEST THOMSON

ABOVE
Richard
Attenborough
with Margot
Fonteyn and
Nureyev

RIGHT
Joan Hammond

LEFT
Julian Bream

Malcolm Arnold

I didn't know how to account for the whole of the hour I had been absent. There was a visitor at the flat when I got back but, to my intense embarrassment, Gilbert demanded to know what Lord Horder had said. Fortunately, the visitor was on the point of leaving, so I was able to postpone my report a little longer. But then I had to begin my tale. To my startled dismay, I had told him no more than that Lord Horder was very dissatisfied with his progress and blamed himself for not making him enter a nursing home, when I burst into tears. This so moved Gilbert that he never asked to hear more. He could not know that my tears were as much for the sad, worried old man I had left as for Gilbert himself.

Lord Horder died only a few months after Gilbert's recovery and although I had not seen him for some time, I felt I had lost a friend. While he was attending Gilbert he told us that in the autumn he was to make the Week's Good Cause appeal for Wireless for the Bedridden and jokingly announced his intention of raising more money than Gilbert's appeal, two years earlier, had raised. When the doctor died, Gilbert was asked to make the appeal in his place and, as I have told earlier, he raised over a thousand pounds more than on the previous occasion.

For the last weeks of his treatment, Gilbert did try quite hard to behave and, apart from a few minor lapses, he succeeded. But it was always difficult to control the flow of visitors and it was hard to blame him for allowing them to stay too long when I found them as interesting and stimulating as he did himself. John Betjeman came several times; his tremendous enthusiasms rather unnerved me when I first knew him and it was some time before I could be at ease in his company. John Pudney, poet, author and publisher, called often and so did Margaret Rawlings, the actress, who told immensely funny stories of her early experiences in the theatre. John Clements and his wife, Kay Hammond, both brilliant conversationalists, arrived one day and, on another, Ian Carmichael, who is as lively and amusing off the screen as on it. One of the most memorable visits was that of Hannen Swaffer, for whom Gilbert had a great respect and who treated Gilbert as though he were a promising young man. Mr. Swaffer is very deaf and so conversations with him tend to become monologues by Hannen Swaffer. He had somehow got hold of the idea that Gilbert was suffering from alcoholism. Gilbert's protests went unheard.

'Give it up, Gilbert! Give it up! If I could, you can,' roared Swaff. It seemed that a long time ago in his career as a theatre critic, he had had to be almost carried home after every first night. But he had taken some course of treatment and never touched a drink since. As he left, Mr. Swaffer was still counselling courage and perseverance and somewhere in the picture library of *The People* there must still be a picture of Swaff, finger raised in awful warning, admonishing Gilbert to 'Give it up!'

After two months of complete confinement indoors, Gilbert was at last allowed to go out. A friend of his was ill in hospital and Gilbert decided that his first outing would be a visit to him. This seemed such a sensible and gentle outing that, after he had left the flat shortly after six o'clock, I was able to go home, in the belief that all was now well, to enjoy my first complete evening of freedom for nine weeks. As I let myself into the Weymouth Street flat at nine o'clock the following morning, the radiogram was playing loudly. But not loudly enough to drown the noise of several cheerful voices coming from the sitting-room. George, the driver of the car Gilbert had bought a few months before, met me in the hall. He told me that Gilbert had been out all night, that he had arrived home only a few minutes earlier, very drunk, with four men from Fleet Street. My heart and mind seemed to turn over. It was a small relief, when I went into the room and was introduced, to find that the men from Fleet Street were not reporters but printers whom Gilbert had met in one of the Covent Garden public houses, where drinks can be served in the early morning and where they were refreshing themselves on their way home from the night shift. But Gilbert was, indeed, very drunk, and it was late in the afternoon before he had sobered sufficiently to tell me as much of his first outing as he could remember. An evening newspaper had already told me part of the story. Seen by a journalist in a well-known Bond Street night-club, Gilbert had, with more than usual acumen, offered the explanation that he was 'killing time before going to Waterloo to meet his aunt who was arriving by an early morning train'. From that day his life, socially at any rate, was back to normal.

A fortnight later, after he and I had spent a few days of comfort and peace at the lovely Gloucestershire home of his old friend Colonel Robert Henriques, Gilbert left for a six weeks' motoring holiday in France and Spain to complete his recovery. Gilbert, George and the car were taken by air ferry to Le Touquet and

Gilbert insisted that, just for fun, I should go with them, have lunch in Le Touquet and fly back the same afternoon. It was a splendid treat – save for two things. We had forgotten that in winter French time is one hour ahead of ours, and so my lunch had to be briefer and more hurried than we had intended. And I did not know that a swift trip of that kind does not permit of Customs concessions. The half-bottle of liqueur brandy I had bought in Le Touquet cost me, therefore, ten shillings more than it would have done in London and the hundred cigarettes I had bought on the plane worked out at about five shillings for twenty. My mind, already confused by a delicious and expensive lunch, with beautiful wines, was further bemused when, because of the difference in British and French time, I discovered that we touched down at Lydd thirty-five minutes before I had taken off from Le Touquet!

While he was away I received the usual occasional postcard, telephone call and letter – all full of instructions. One of these letters I still have. It starts:

'April 1st or is it? Anyhow, it's Friday.

We are about to set off for Barcelona. The idea now is to find a quiet *pension* or small hotel north of Barcelona – on the Costa Brava – and there to spend next week (Holy Week) in peace and quiet.

It'll be a nice change from driving and from "luxury" hotels. (Ha Ha!) Not that there's been anything to grumble much at really – and most of it *vastly* amusing.

George *can* laugh and has a not altogether unsuspected sense of humour.

This 'ere missive is to ask certain questions because I always forget what to say on the telephone.

1. Was Uncle Walter in D. Nixon's show?
2. Are you getting the bedroom cupboard papered?
3. What about X – I think we proceed. I've been thinking and I'm tired of being diddled. Geo will go and get radio from Peckham when he gets back.
4. Rent?
5. Bill – TV set?
6. Please find out from Esmé Percy the name, address and t. no. of his friends in Paris whom I met at the Club. I want to know this *very* particularly. George wants v. much to go to Paris and

I think it's a pity that he shouldn't go up the Eiffel Tower and down the Metro (his ambitions). But by that time we may need dough and a place to stay quietly.

7. It appears that Mrs. T. gave X a good radio set which he has sold (given away). He must give her a Burgundy.

8. Please send £4 in cash, registered envelope, to Mrs. X with a note to say it comes at George's request from abroad. The father may be in hospital and she may be a bit short.

9. Ask David D. to enquire about a Fleetwood Ford through Pratts. I believe they are only made in Chiswick.

10. Write me a long letter on airmail paper ready for sending as soon as I can give you an address.

Be a good boy.

Love to all,

G.H.'

It can be seen that my employer was not one who delegates responsibility, not a man with a single-track mind, not someone who can ever really relax. I can still laugh about the flood of instructions he sent from Ireland in 1959 about the new dining-room carpet. On the ninth of July he wrote: 'I like the red sisal, but Joan says it quarrels with the pink in the curtains, whereas the green will tone very nicely. So let it be the green and if it could be done by July 22nd *tant mieux*.' On 10th July he sent a postcard saying: 'Could we not tack sisal all over dining-room floor, leaving space for door to open?' Later the same day, heading his postcard 10/7/59 (No. 2), he gave up: 'Just re-read your letter. Better to hold carpet consideration till we can talk it over properly. So NO ACTION please.' I particularly liked 'could *we* not tack the sisal . . .' He knew and I knew, and he knew that I knew, that he would not know which end of the hammer to hold!

Although Gilbert's schedule was planned for a six weeks' holiday in France and Spain, I felt it unlikely that he would stay away so long. The exciting novelty of being an unknown, ordinary tourist would soon wear off and, without the stimulus either of public admiration or intellectual conversation (for he spoke no Spanish), Gilbert would find himself perpetually face to face with the only company he dreaded – his own. I had a great deal of work to catch up with at this time and, in addition, I travelled home to Yorkshire every weekend to visit my mother, who was

seriously ill in hospital. So I was very disappointed, but not surprised, when rather less than four weeks after his departure Gilbert
telephoned me from Paris one Sunday to say that he would be
home the following day.

He returned to start a new programme. The *Harding Interviews*
on sound radio had not been an unqualified success, but he himself and the B B C were still trying to find a way to dissociate
him from being a purely panel participant. So *Harding Finds Out*,
on television, was the next step. For this programme Gilbert had two
assistants – Peter Baker (at that time one of the team of journalists
engaged on the 'Ephraim Hardcastle' column in the *Sunday
Express*) and Jacqueline Mackenzie (an actress who, after training
in repertory, had played small parts in television plays). The object
of the programme, as announced in the *Radio Times*, was that
Gilbert should investigate all kinds of questions and situations,
ranging from 'Why are railway carriages dirty?' to 'Who *really*
killed the Princes in the Tower?' Many of the questions asked
had been raised by him before, not only in broadcasts but in his
People column. Few of them were fresh enough to stand several
minutes' demonstration and discussion on the television screen. The
first instalment was badly received by the newspaper critics. 'Gilbert's T V fireworks are damp squibs,' said the *Daily Sketch*,
describing the programme as 'rigid, unimaginative and downright
lazy. Harding himself did little or no finding out.' The *Daily
Express* said the programme 'lacked original controversy, it lacked
pace, it lacked bite, it lacked humour and humanity. It also lacked
material from the enlisted viewers. "We *would* like sensible questions," pleaded the docile Harding. And no wonder.' Only Peter
Black, the *Daily Mail* critic, liked the programme. His enthusiastic
notice was headlined 'Harding finds his best line. The new Gilbert
is T V success.'

Though it started off so coldly, the series did gain momentum
as it went along. Some of the problems it raised were questions
that mattered very much to the ordinary viewer. But it did not
establish, as Gilbert and the B B C had hoped, a new level for
Harding in broadcast entertainment of a more serious kind. If
it achieved nothing spectacular, however, it did bring Jackie Mackenzie into our lives for a space. Intelligent, gay, good-looking and
warm-hearted, she rose rapidly to fame in television until she left
it on her marriage. Alas, I understood only too well when Gilbert
said one evening, just as she had left us, 'Isn't she all that is

charming and delightful? That is exactly the kind of woman I would like to marry.'

There were other interesting and exciting encounters for me that summer. At a party he gave to discuss the yearly charity production *Night of a Hundred Stars*, I first met Noël Coward. And I was introduced to Beatrice Lillie, Margaret Leighton, Vivien Leigh and Sir Laurence Olivier, Laurence Harvey, Hermione Baddeley, and dozens of other glittering stars I had long admired. I had been shy of meeting Mr. Coward, but it was, of course, unnecessary. He knew exactly how to put me – and his fifty other guests – completely at ease. The reason for my shyness, I suppose, was the story that Gilbert was so fond of telling about him. Gilbert had, it seemed, fallen asleep and snored rather loudly (and unmistakably) at the first night of Mr. Coward's play *Quadrille*. It was not the sort of behaviour that a playwright could overlook, so Gilbert had some embarrassment at their next meeting. He started at once to apologize and explain, but his protestations were gracefully interrupted. 'Think nothing of it, my dear fellow,' said Noël Coward, with his taut smile. 'You can be quite sure that I have never bored you half as much as you have bored me.' But despite his barbed tongue, he is obviously a thoughtful and kind man for, more than a year later, when I met him again at the Café de Paris with Gilbert, I was charmed to find that he remembered my name.

Gilbert's first family visitor then came to stay for a few days at Weymouth Street. His mother's sister, 'Aunt Edie', came down from Hereford on her first visit to London for sixty years. It was a great occasion for them both. Gilbert took her to theatres and cinemas, to television shows and radio broadcasts, and to lunch and dine in the smartest hotels and restaurants. What thrilled her most of all was when her photograph with Gilbert was published in some of the Sunday newspapers. What most enchanted *him* was his vicarious pleasure in her first visit to the Ritz Hotel which, she believed, did not exist outside smart novels. It was quite obvious, when Gilbert saw her off from London, that his beloved aunt had had the time of her life!

That summer, too, Marlene Dietrich returned to London and the Café de Paris. Gilbert was enchanted when he was one of the first people she got in touch with: though it was not so surprising, since he had sent a wonderful bouquet of flowers to greet her arrival at the Dorchester. That year Miss Dietrich's cabaret act was introduced by a different well-known woman each night, and I was overjoyed when Nancy Spain invited me, as well as Gilbert, to be her guest when her turn came. I had heard so much from Gilbert and others of Marlene's enchantment that I might easily have been disappointed. But I wasn't; I was overwhelmed. And later, when we went with Nancy to her dressing-room, the spell was unbroken. A few nights later Gilbert and I went to the Café de Paris again, when Lady Barnett made the introduction and we were both delighted when, towards the end of the evening, Miss Dietrich joined us for a few minutes at our table.

Before she returned to the States, Gilbert arranged to give a small party for her at the Weymouth Street flat – 'about twenty people, I should think', he suggested. In the end, of course, there were nearer sixty; all the people to whom Gilbert really wanted to give great pleasure – as, it was obvious, he did – he could not resist asking along to meet Marlene Dietrich. There were Mr. and Mrs. John Betjeman, the late Lord Carisbrooke and Lady Carisbrooke, Uncle Walter Harding and his wife, John Foster, Q.C., Kate Wadleigh, Leslie Jackson (producer of *What's My Line?* and *This is Your Life*), Jacqueline Mackenzie, and Sir Bernard and Lady Docker.

Gilbert's old friend, Mrs. Bessie Braddock, M P, was also invited, but House of Commons business prevented her coming – fortunately, perhaps for Gilbert's peace of mind. Lady Docker and Mrs. Braddock had each taken their turn, as famous women, to introduce Miss Dietrich's act at the Café de Paris, Mrs. Braddock only on the eve of the party. The next day's newspapers had fully reported a slight scene at the Café. Lady Docker, who was there, had been obliged by the restaurant's rules to take her party to a balcony table, instead of to the dance floor, because she was not wearing evening dress. On the cue for the cabaret, Mrs. Bessie Braddock took her place on the rostrum to welcome the artist – and she was wearing a navy-blue suit. Lady Docker swept out of the Café, vowing she would never return to it. As it was, at Gilbert's party her arrival caused an undercurrent of difficulty, for she came just as Marlene was leaving. The host thus found himself in the position of not knowing whether he should stay to welcome Lady Docker or take his guest of honour to her car. It was Miss Dietrich herself who solved the problem, by whispering to Gilbert, 'Anyone can see me to my car. You must stay with Norah, poor thing.'

Soon after the party came the midnight performance at the

Palladium of the *Night of a Hundred Stars* – a night I shall never forget. Gilbert and Jack Hawkins, in uniform, acted as doormen outside the theatre, and later Gilbert was one of the many celebrities who formed the 'audience' on stage for the cabaret scene which formed the second half of the show. Gilbert shared a dressing-room with Douglas Byng, John Gregson, Dickie Henderson, Bobby Howes, Terence Morgan, Robert Beatty, Brian Reece – and the six members of the Crazy Gang. After helping the 'doorman' to change into a dinner-jacket, I tried to make myself generally useful to anyone in the room who needed help, for several of them had to make quick changes. My efforts might have been more effective had it not been for the effervescence of the Crazy Gang. Whatever I happened to put down for a second – collar-studs, cuff-links, make-up, or clothing – was whisked away by one or other of them. Then, with bland innocence, they would try to convince me that I was the crazy one. But I must have been of some assistance, for when the show was over, at about 5 a.m., Brian Reece tried to tip me. I realized then that they had not known I was Gilbert's secretary but supposed I had been hired to help behind the scenes. Too late, I knew that I should have pocketed the money and just said 'Thank you'. Instead I tried to explain and in a moment poor Mr. Reece was as hot under the collar as I was myself. Later Bobby Howes came over to thank me and to say good night. After shaking his hand I found that a ten-shilling note had been transferred to mine. This time I kept silent.

After his return from holiday in France and Spain, Gilbert had fallen quickly into his old routine. His consumption of alcohol had risen to its pre-Horder level, and by the end of the summer he had regained all the weight previously lost. Once more he travelled all over the country, fulfilling engagements of one kind and another. Once again he got into newspaper headlines. This time it was because of an honestly held and frankly expressed opinion of our imperial past. In *Who Said That?* he had called the Empire 'an unhappy, unwholesome, and evil thing. . . . We were, God forgive us, a greedy, grasping people. That is all over now. There is a difference between the Empire and the Commonwealth. The Empire has gone: and good riddance!' Referring to his own stay in Cyprus, he spoke of 'chinless idiots lording it over their superiors'. Such a storm arose! The *Daily Express*, the *Daily Mail*, and the *Yorkshire Post* condemned him in their leading articles. The *Daily Mail* ran feature page articles on two consecutive days and carried columns of readers' letters for days after. Not a little confusion arose in the public mind because this was about the time of the announcement that Field-Marshal Sir John Harding was about to take up his post as Governor of Cyprus. But the words 'Harding' and 'Cyprus' together, to a great many readers meant Gilbert and his phrase 'chinless idiots'. The *Mail* commented on this with a cartoon showing Gilbert reading a copy of that newspaper bearing the headline 'Strong-man Harding for Cyprus'. The caption of the cartoon just said, 'Not you, Gilbert – sit down!'

The B B C announced that *What's My Line?* would return to the screen that autumn. Though by now Gilbert was thoroughly bored with that programme, he felt he couldn't afford not to be on the panel, and the thought of another winter spent in weekly attempts to discover the occupations of 'people I have never met, never want to meet and whose dreary occupations bore me abysmally' depressed him deeply. The strain of long journeys and irregular hours began to exhaust him, and once again I knew the feeling of living on the edge of a rumbling volcano.

It was then that some friends told him of miraculous cures wrought on them by a homoeopathic doctor and, to the astonished dismay of myself and others, he decided to consult him. Much impressed at a first meeting, he agreed to undergo the prescribed treatment, and for the second time that year started on a strict diet and a rigid control of his drinking. The diet was largely a vegetarian one and he was encouraged to eat all the vegetables, salads and fruit he could face. Instead of gin or whisky, it was suggested he try freshly made fruit- and vegetable-juice drinks. And there was a vast array of pills, powders and tablets to be taken regularly throughout the day. Perhaps the most startling prescription of all was that he should take plenty of walking exercise.

Diana Roberts was an enormous help in all this. She had once lived on a vegetarian diet and it was she who now prepared most of his food and drinks and organized his exercise. Each morning for several weeks she arrived at Weymouth Street shortly after seven and she, Gilbert, and Cham-Pu the Pekinese (a recent gift from Mrs. Robert Henriques), would set off to Regent's Park, about a quarter of a mile away. It was on one of these walks that Gilbert encountered an old and appropriately dirty tramp in the park. He insisted on taking him back, talking happily all the way, to the flat, where he was given the use of his bath, a hearty breakfast (cooked by Diana), and five pounds to help him on his way. Diana was greatly amused to find that Gilbert had drawn the line at letting the tramp use his own razor, but had lent him instead one belonging to a friend who was using the spare room at the time.

At this time he was determined to find a house in the country for his leisure time, but meanwhile he took, on a six months' lease, a furnished flat in Hove. Although he was seldom able to spend more than two days at a time there, Gilbert fell in love with Brighton and with the Downs behind it, and eventually abandoned the idea of a house in the country. In a remarkably short time he found in Montpelier Villas, Brighton, exactly the house he wanted and his solicitor began negotiations for its purchase. Gilbert was very pleased and excited about it.

But unfortunately that did not help to strengthen his health resolutions. He just could not find the self-discipline to stick rigidly to his diet, or to avoid alcohol, and there were many grave lapses. Perhaps it was because of this, or perhaps because the treatment itself was unsuitable, but it became clear that Gilbert's physical condition was deteriorating rapidly. At this stage he was having twice-daily injections of fluid – which George and I had been taught to give, with reluctance on our part and a most reassuring bravery on his. 'Specimens' had to be submitted daily to a homoeopathic chemist near Oxford Street, and it was Gilbert's fixed and blithely expressed opinion that these formed the source of fluid for the injections. But he was rapidly becoming even more breathless than I had previously known. His face took on an ominous purple tinge and, even to my untrained way of thinking, it seemed that his ever-increasing bulk was due to the fact that his body was retaining too much fluid. His legs and ankles became so swollen that it was painful to see them. He was unable himself to put on socks and slippers, and it filled me with pity to have to ease them on so gently and carefully. The walking exercise became quite impossible.

I could feel that he was himself becoming frightened, and this, of course, exacerbated his temper. Almost every day there were tremendous scenes, usually about nothing at all. One day Diana returned from shopping with a bag laden with fruit and vegetables and crowned with a large bunch of bananas. Gilbert roared:

'Good heavens, woman, what are those for? I am sick to nausea of the sight of that flabby, flocculent fruit! I loathe bananas. I have always loathed bananas. Don't let me ever see one again! Anyway, we've already got some.'

'That's all right,' said Diana, as calmly as she could. I'll have the bananas then,' and took a ten-shilling note out of her purse.

'And what's that for – if I may be so bold as to ask?'

'For the bananas,' said Diana.

With a yell of, 'How dare you insult me?' Gilbert grabbed the bunch and the note, rushed to the open window and hurled them to the street below. Unknown to him, the ten-shilling note fluttered back into the room, was covered by my foot and quietly handed back to Diana. As I thrust my head from the window, I managed to see that the bananas had landed on top of a car parked three floors below.

Diana and I stayed silent. Then, quite calmly, Gilbert called George. As he appeared, 'Oh, George,' he said, 'we've just dropped a bunch of bananas out of the window. Be a good boy – run down and pick them up, would you?'

George reached the pavement in time to see the car, decorated like a tropical harvest festival, just moving off towards Oxford Circus.

A few days later there was another tremendous scene when Gilbert, unjustifiably, accused me of 'answering him back'. In his fury he kicked at the table on which I had just set down a cup of coffee for him. His shin made sharp contact with the edge of the table and, though the cup and saucer remained in place, the coffee shot into the air, drenching all the letters and papers on the table. The cascade of abuse continued until he left, late in the afternoon, to spend a few days in Gloucestershire. When he had been gone for about half an hour and the nervous sweat was beginning to dry on me, the phone rang. It was Gilbert, continuing the storm of condemnation where he had left off. Another half hour passed, and he telephoned again, still in the same vein. Perhaps two hours later, as he rang for the sixth time, he said: 'Poor Podge, are you *still* in the office? I never expected to find you still at it, at this hour. Really, it is so inconsiderate of me. You know, dear boy, you must learn to control your temper and not set me off on a great tirade like this. You must learn to be patient with me, Roger, mustn't you?'

'Yes,' I said weakly. 'I'll try to do my best.'

After he came back from Gloucestershire, the next journey was to Cardiff to take part in a television programme there. It worried me a great deal, and I was surprised that Gilbert should accept the opinion of his homoeopathic adviser that his increasingly hampered movement was a sign that the cure was working. But though he insisted on my accompanying him, the patient was apparently quite confident. We took the train to South Wales on a bitterly cold day towards the end of November and it was obvious to me that his health deteriorated even during that day. By the evening his legs were swelling visibly, so that he could barely walk, and every movement made him breathless. I felt sick at heart. We decided to telephone the homoeopathic doctor, who advised a double dose of all the pills and assured me that Mr. Harding would be well by the following morning. We went to the hotel that had been booked for the night, but by this time we were both so frightened that I heartily welcomed Gilbert's suggestion that we should drive straight back to London. We hired a car and started off. It was the most dreadful drive of my life. Because he could barely breathe, Gilbert asked me to wind down both windows. Through the dim night hours from Cardiff to London, we drove furiously, with the bitter air whipping round us. I believed I should never be warm again.

Back at Weymouth Street, with not the least compunction, I telephoned to Gilbert's own orthodox doctor. He came, examined him, and was shocked. He immediately arranged an appointment with an eminent heart specialist for that afternoon. But between the examination and the appointment, Gilbert was due to give a lunch-time lecture at *The Sunday Times* Book Exhibition at the Royal Festival Hall. And, as it was expected of him, he did so. Diana and I went with him and, when the lecture was over, we heard him accept an invitation to lunch at the Caprice. But he returned in time for his appointment with the specialist, Dr. Paul Wood, and, a few hours later, was in bed at the Brompton Hospital.

There he stayed for four weeks. It was largely a repetition of his stay at the clinic. Drugs, administered normally at first, had to be increased to inhuman proportions to achieve their effect. The patient's demands for books, fruit, and unseasonable delicacies sent me scurrying hourly backwards and forwards. His *People* column was dictated to Kate between the ministrations of doctors and nurses. A television set was installed, rejected, and installed again.

The day before Christmas Eve he returned home where, according to the newspaper reports, he would 'spend Christmas very quietly'. I left for my own holidays with my parents in Yorkshire with little hope that this report would be authentic.

CHAPTER TEN

INTERLUDE FOR WORK

WHEN I came back to work after the Christmas holiday, I found chaos. But it wasn't Gilbert's fault. He had had trouble with his new driver, who had left by the time I returned.

Gilbert's cars so often brought trouble. It was in 1954 that he first bought one: though it was not, in fact, the first car he had owned. Thirty years before he had had a car which he drove himself but, when it broke down one day on a road near Portsmouth, he gave up being a motorist. There was a garage a few yards down the road. Gilbert trudged along to it and asked: 'What will you give me for that car?' For the cost of a hired car to Portsmouth and a five-pound note the vehicle changed hands. After that, as he himself often said, he decided that neither his temper nor his manners were good enough to permit him to have control of such a lethal weapon.

So when he got the Ford Zephyr-Zodiac we first had to find a driver: not a 'chauffeur', that was much too pretentious a word. We put an advertisement in one of the London evening newspapers. But, quite by coincidence, the morning after it had appeared, Gilbert received a letter from a man in the north who said that, on the death of his employer, his job as houseman-valet had ended and offered his services to Gilbert. 'That is a coincidence we cannot ignore,' he said. 'Send him a telegram and ask him to telephone to me.' That was on a Saturday. By the time I arrived at Weymouth Street on the Monday morning, my employer had had one of his high-pressure organizing spasms. The applicant had come to London, been interviewed, engaged, and sent back to Oldham to pack his possessions and return on Tuesday.

'Well, that's fine,' I said. 'He must be good.'

'Yes, yes, of course,' said Gilbert. 'He was with Sir X— Y—, been with him for years. That's recommendation enough. Nice, honest northerner, with a fine Lancashire accent.' Gilbert, who could adopt almost any accent he chose at will, was speaking with Oldham's flatness and a winning smile on his face. I sensed that something was wrong and I waited.

'There's just one thing,' he added, when he saw I expected more, 'he hasn't, in fact, got a driver's licence.'

'But—'

'Oh, I know, I know. We'll get him a quick course of lessons – he did drive in the army during the war – and that'll be all right.'

So we arranged for driving lessons. While the car stood idle, the 'driver' pressed suits and helped in the flat and took a lesson every day. And he became more and more nervous. He was, quite obviously, used to a placid household. Privately his driving instructor told me that, while his nerves were so frayed, he could never hope to become a good driver. Poor man; he was so obviously unhappy that it was no surprise to me when Gilbert telephoned to me at home one Saturday afternoon to say he had come home to find a note from his driver on the kitchen table. It said, quite simply, that he felt he had made a great mistake in ever taking on the job, that he couldn't face having to work out his notice, and had gone back north.

Once more the advertisement was sent to the evening papers. This time, among many applicants, it produced George – an excellent driver, and a patient man. Though he decided at least three times that he could no longer put up with the difficulties of working for Gilbert, he served in all about eighteen months. The next driver, too, lasted about the same length of time and then left to get married and enjoy a quiet home life. After that came a succession of others: some stayed for three months, some for as many weeks. Two left after only a few days, and one disappeared overnight, never to be heard of again. Their main difficulty – and ours – was, of course, that driving in this case was not a full-time job and what was needed was someone who could be a bit of a cook, a bit of a handyman, a good valet, and a first-class driver, which is a difficult post to advertise, or to fill. Eventually, and privately, I awarded a Harding Long Service Medal to anyone who stayed twelve months. Such a one was David Watkins, his last driver, the only member of Gilbert's household to be with him when he died.

The driver who left while I was spending Christmas in Yorkshire had been engaged while Gilbert was in the Brompton Hospital, on the recommendation of a Roman Catholic priest who was a friend of Gilbert's. He had told us quite frankly that this man had been to Borstal as a youth but was now completely reformed and reliable. Because of a war injury, the slightest amount of alcohol affected him swiftly but, fortunately, he had such an aversion to the stuff that there was no risk of trouble in that form. During the holiday Gilbert suggested that he might like an evening off and told him he could take the car, so long as he was back by midnight, because they were due to start early in the morning to visit a friend in the country. By two o'clock there was no sign of car or driver, and Gilbert began to get very worried. Eventually, unable to calm himself, he went down and out into the street to see if, perhaps, the car was round the corner. He looked in all directions and was suddenly horrified to see a car, coming at great speed, cross the red traffic lights. Careering from one side of the road to the other, it eventually pulled up against the opposite pavement. It was his car and his driver. With some difficulty, Gilbert helped the poor, helplessly intoxicated man out of the car and into the lift and persuaded him into bed. The following morning a short, sharp exchange had terminated that driver's employment.

The next search ended with Gilbert's engaging two men. The first, Arthur Deeley, though an experienced driver, had never been in private employment before, but he was kind and willing and earned my private Order. . . . 'Brother' Deeley was what Gilbert constantly called him. It was vivid evidence of that side of Gilbert Harding which revolted against a master-and-man relationship. In his boyhood, when in Hereford caps were still touched to the gentry, Gilbert had been one of the cap-touchers; as an intelligent child, he had rebelled, for basically he believed in the equality of man, and, as a grown man, he knew of no reason why one who was paid thousands of pounds to entertain the public should be able to command the servility of another who performed a useful service.

There were quite a few people who said he was a snob. It was true that he openly delighted in the company of aristocracy, and would put himself to a great deal of trouble to accept the invitations of members of ancient families who sought his acquaintance. But, as far as he could, he also forbade any publicity about such occasions. Many a time, had he been the ordinary run of gossip columnist, he could have filled his *People* column with stories of a weekend with Lord X or a dinner party with the Duchess of Y.

But he could never bring himself to do so. I believe it was his innate love of tradition that made him relish the nobility. He knew by heart the ancient titles of England. He would recite them on the least provocation:

'Bernard Marmaduke Fitzalan-Howard, Duke of Norfolk, Earl Marshal and Hereditary Marshal and Chief Butler of England, Earl of Arundel, Baron Maltravers, Earl of Surrey, Baron Fitzalan, Clun and Oswaldestre, Earl of Norfolk and Baron Herries . . .' would come rolling off his tongue like a litany. And it sounded splendid, great and noble, like a passage from Shakespeare.

But his feeling for the great never conditioned his manner to the less. When he was himself, he never demanded service: he asked, politely, for it. So when, after his spell in the Brompton Hospital, with Gilbert's health recovered and his temper mild, 'Brother' Deeley and the cook-houseman joined us, the household began to run smoothly again. Even though, after a few weeks, the latter had to return to the north of England, a happy routine had been established. Over six months passed in almost uninterrupted calm – perhaps the most happy period of my employment.

This may have been because at that time all of us were so absorbed in the preparation of Gilbert's new Brighton home. We were as much infected by his hesitations as by his enthusiasms. He would have liked to choose and supervise all the decoration and the furnishing of the house. He might, with difficulty, have found the time to do so, but his tastes had been influenced by such diverse backgrounds as the workhouse, the Wolverhampton Orphans' School, and his Cambridge college friends, and so he did not have sufficient confidence in his own judgement. So all the basic decorations and furnishing had been put into the hands of a friend who was an interior decorator and antique dealer. Even while his client was in hospital, this friend would call on him, bringing samples of wallpapers, carpet and fabrics, and Gilbert, safe in the knowledge that all these were 'in good taste', was happy to make his own selections.

Within a few weeks of actually buying the house, he had carefully and, with much consideration, bought a few small items of furniture. But it was obvious that, at that rate, it would take months to furnish the whole house, with its eleven rooms, of which three in the basement formed a separate flat. Eventually, he gave the antique dealer a free hand to do it more or less as he thought it should be. Then, when all was in place, such items as did not please Gilbert were changed. It was a fairly swift and effective method and the result was attractive and in perfect taste. But, to me, it never really appeared to be a home: it lacked true individuality and, probably, a few examples of dull utility. Even the many stains which the untrained and untrainable Cham-Pu made on almost every carpet and chair failed to give the place a lived-in feeling.

But it could have been very much worse. Soon after it became known that Gilbert had bought a house in Brighton, the proprietors of a famous women's magazine approached him with the suggestion that they should completely furnish it for him at their expense. This was to give them the exclusive right to photograph it for regular features in the magazine and to change the decorations and furnishings as often as they wished. Gilbert, like anyone else, loved to get something for nothing, but I was quite astounded when I found that he was seriously considering this offer. It was only because he insisted that he must retain his gas cooker and refrigerator and the few pieces of furniture he had already chosen, and a particular striped wallpaper already planned for the sitting-room that the offer was finally withdrawn. He was bitterly disappointed, and though I tried hard to convince him that living in a permanent exhibition would have been hideously unrestful he would not be comforted.

At this time, too, he was busy with much writing. His *Picture Post* contract had come to an end and now he had a general column in *John Bull*, as well as his *People* column, and, in fulfilment of a promise made to Joan Werner-Laurie on the trip to Jamaica, when she started her new monthly magazine *She*, Gilbert had a half-page at the end to comment on the other contents. That year the *Evening Standard* ran a murder mystery serial called *The 'What's My Line?' Murder*. It was written by Julian Symons with Gilbert's close collaboration, which took quite a lot of his time.

In addition he was also preparing his second book, *The Book of Manners*, which was published that autumn. Like his previous book, this was dictated to a journalist, though not to the same one, and Gilbert made his own corrections and additions to the final manuscript. It was an amusing and entertaining book – a comment on good and bad manners – but its sales fell far short of the earlier one, *Along My Line*. This was mainly due to the fact that it was published only a few days after *The Gilbert Harding Question Book*, from another publisher, which sold well. For that one, compiled by a Manchester schoolmaster, Gilbert was paid an outright fee for the use of his name: for his own book, he drew royalties, but more than these went as a fee to the journalist concerned.

The situation became even more ironic when, on his way back from Manchester, where he had been signing copies of both books at a large store, his car was involved in an accident a few miles outside Oxford. Three vehicles were involved, with little damage to any of them, but it did not seem clear whose fault it had been. Unfortunately, the police decided to prosecute Deeley, Gilbert's driver. He was fined £20 and had his licence suspended for three months. Notice of appeal was given and, in the meantime, Deeley was allowed to continue driving. We were all shocked, when the appeal was heard some months later, to find the suspension increased from three months to six.

This was the second accident in which Gilbert's car had been involved. Earlier in the year there had been a collision with a motor-cycle in which the rider had been injured. There was no prosecution, but the motor-cyclist successfully claimed substantial damages. During the next few years there were more accidents, though none serious enough to cause injury. But our long-suffering insurance company finally rebelled. They had paid out nearly £4,000 against his premiums of just over £300. The company stiffly increased the premiums, so that by the time Gilbert owned two cars he was paying more than £5 a week for insurance, and they made a stipulation that he should pay the first £150 of any repair bill.

Since Gilbert did not drive himself it would be unfair to say he was responsible for most of them, but a good deal of the blame nevertheless lay with him. He was a dangerous passenger. Oddly, he loved speed and could not bear his car to be overtaken. 'Faster, faster, Brother Deeley. Are you going to trundle along behind that ancient monument for ever?' If he had been drinking, he did not hesitate to lean over and bang his fist on the horn. Sometimes he would slump, asleep, on to the driver's shoulder, and it was almost impossible to ease his dead weight back on to his own side of the car. Luckily, in each car he insisted on an arm-rest between the front passenger and the driver and, though it was installed for his own comfort, I have no doubt it prevented many an accident.

Another of his failings as a passenger was to give directions. No matter how well the driver might know the route, Gilbert always insisted he knew a better one. Even when he was wide awake, his directions were unreliable. 'Right at the next fork,' he would say firmly, and then, as the driver started to turn, 'Left, you momentous idiot! Left, I said,' and the poor man would find himself stuck in the middle of the crossing. It was always possible, too, that he would fall asleep in the middle of the drive, after starting the journey on some route which only he knew. Once, returning from London to Brighton, he decided to try a new way someone had described to him. He got the driver thoroughly lost and slipped into a deep sleep. More than an hour later he woke up to find himself in Rye – almost as far away from Brighton as when they had left London. When he first had the car I very often used to accompany him, but these tactics terrified me, alone in the back seat and sweating with tension. So I started a campaign to convince him that, while I was perfectly happy in a train, road-travel made me car-sick. To my astonishment and delight, he gradually came to accept this, and my hours of agony were considerably reduced.

There often seemed to be new plans afoot for Gilbert to make records or to appear in plays, on the stage and on television, but few of them came to fruition. In the summer of 1956 one of the smaller recording companies announced with a blaze of publicity that he would play the part of Toad in a long-playing record of *Toad of Toad Hall* from Kenneth Grahame's *The Wind in the Willows*. Gilbert was very enthusiastic. He practised a great, gravelly voice and, on the most unsuitable occasions, would suddenly burst out: 'O bliss! O poop-poop! O my! The poetry of motion! Here today – in next week tomorrow! . . .' But, as always if there was any delay in his plans, he became impatient. And with impatience his enthusiasm waned. When the record was finally issued, the part of Toad was played by, I believe, Norman Shelley.

A few months later another company announced that they would record *Peter and the Wolf*, with Gilbert as narrator. It was recorded without delay, but both Gilbert and the company were dissatisfied with the result. Parts of it were re-recorded, but before it was finally issued the company went into liquidation. Later the rights of the record were bought by another company, but Gilbert was still too displeased with it to give permission for it to be sold to the public. One reasonably successful record, which he had made earlier with Hermione Gingold, had somewhat astonishingly been banned by the B B C. On one side the pair unmelodiously sang *Two to Tango*: on the other – the banned one – was *Oh, Grandma*. a version of 'Red Riding Hood'. I never heard the official reason for it, but Gilbert's story was that the B B C considered one of the ludicrously passionate asides, spoken between the lines of the song, as obscene. Gilbert murmured, 'Oh, Hermione, can I have you for a regular diet?' to which she replied huskily, 'Yes, Gilbert, but don't speak with your mouth full!' Later he also recorded one of the songs from Walt Disney's *Peter Pan* in aid of a children's charity and, most successfully of all, a version of *Three Blind Mice*, in which he was accompanied by his Uncle Walter on the contra-bassoon.

The Man Who Came to Dinner was the play idea that constantly haunted him. It was a 'natural' for Gilbert Harding. He did at one time very seriously consider appearing in it for a theatrical company. The salary they offered was very big and their confidence in his ability and encouragement to him to start a new line tempted him. They planned that the play should open with a long provincial tour, to allow Gilbert to adjust himself to the new medium, and then be brought into the West End. Very wisely, but with reluctance, he finally refused. He appreciated so much better than anyone else his lack of self-discipline. He knew he would quickly become bored with each night-after-night routine detail and unchanging scene. He realized that he would almost certainly try to alleviate the boredom with alcohol, and that would be disastrous. However, when the B B C decided on a television production of the same play, that offered a much more practical proposition. Plans were well advanced when, unhappily, it was discovered that the television rights of the play had been acquired by one of the new companies at that time preparing for the forthcoming independent television opportunities, so there the matter once again ended. Still, the stage rights of the play were freely available, and at least once every six months some theatrical management would approach Gilbert with the brilliant and original suggestion that he should play the leading part. With gleeful malice Gilbert would start: 'Well now, what I *always* say when that suggestion is made to me . . .' and their faces would fall.

It was Miss Joan Littlewood, of Theatre Workshop, who had what seemed to us the most fantastic proposal. Two days after he had been admitted to the Brompton Hospital, it was announced in the press that Miss Littlewood was to stage a production of *Hamlet* and that the name part would be played by Gilbert Harding. A few days earlier she had called on him and made her suggestion. To my utter astonishment Gilbert seemed flattered and interested and agreed to consider the idea. When Miss Littlewood left, my expression must have showed what I felt.

'You think I'm a fool, don't you?' he said sternly. 'Just because you had a great success as a butler on the dusty boards of Little Puddleton's Theatre Royal, you think you're an actor and I'm not! You believe I couldn't play Hamlet, don't you?'

Honesty, I felt, was not just then the best policy. 'No, I'm sure you could,' I said, 'but . . .'

'Then you are a fool. Caught you on the wrong foot, didn't I, Mr. Storey? Hamlet, indeed! You'll have me playing Ariel next.'

'Then why ever did you tell Miss Littlewood you'd think about it?'

'Well, I was so covered with confusion and embarrassment that I thought if I said "No" and she started to argue with me, I might eventually have said "Yes" just to finish it. This way it's easy: we just write and say I have considered it and decided I can't.'

The play was, of course, never produced. But it would, I feel sure, have had a fascinated and bewildered first-night audience, if no more.

Always one of Gilbert's most successful programmes was when he conducted *Housewives' Choice*. He had done so very shortly after I started to work for him and I had been dismayed at the labour such an apparently simple programme involved. It was difficult to persuade Gilbert to knuckle down to it all. But even after the work was finished, his troubles were not over. On the very first morning of the programme he woke at a quarter to nine, more than three-quarters of an hour after the time he was due at the studio for rehearsals and only twenty minutes before he was due on the air. He arrived at the studio just as the signature tune was being played and the announcer was standing by ready to apologize for Gilbert's absence and introduce the records himself.

These programmes brought in hundreds of 'request' postcards, yet each day only between twelve and fourteen could be played, so they had to be selected from about a hundred cards. On each one the name of the music requested and, if suggested, the recording artist, was underlined in red pencil by B B C staff. A high proportion of them, of course, could be rejected right away because the writing was illegible or the sender had forgotten to give the name and address of the person for whom it was to be played, or her own, or sometimes both. Others could be discarded because the music had

not been recorded or had already been played the previous week
or because it was not easy to discover just what was being asked for,
in spite of a long search through catalogues. I remember, for
example, a request for 'Saladaise' and another wanted 'anything by
I. Vorello' – finally translated as 'Salad Days' and 'Ivor Novello'. A
request I shall always remember went something like this:

'Dear Mr. Harding, I wonder if you would play something for
the unknown friend who was so kind to me when I was sick all
over the floor of the ladies' toilet in the gallery of the Garrick
Theatre last Saturday night. She tidied me up and I would be glad
if you would play a record of "Thank you for being an Angle".
P.S. Some people said I was drunk, but I wasn't.'

After the postcards had been sorted and a selection made, came
the job of finding the actual records. If a particular artist's recording had been mentioned it was relatively simple, except when it
was discovered that he had never, in fact, recorded the song. If
none was specified, then a choice often had to be made from many
different recordings of the same music. Then the records had to
be timed so that they would exactly fit the allotted time, and finally
the script had to be written.

Gilbert's taste in music, as in most things, was catholic, but in
the main he preferred the lighter classics. He did receive a few
letters complaining of the dullness of the programmes from people
who would have preferred more 'pop' tunes, but they were outnumbered by at least a hundred to one by those who enjoyed his
selection. It was because of this flood of approval, I imagine,
that the B B C later gave Gilbert his own afternoon programme
on the Light, which was called *Purely for Pleasure* and consisted
entirely of classical music – 'though not *too* classical'. It was the
first time any programme of the kind had been presented on the
Light and its instant and enormous popularity came as a surprise
to us all. It must be said that a great deal of the success, however,
was due to the able producer, John Lade, for the programme came
at a time when Gilbert's disinclination for work had become almost
an inability. All he was expected to do was to choose the titles
he wanted to play (and in this he had the maximum help from
John Lade), to write a brief introduction to each record, and to
read them in the programme. More often than not, Gilbert put
off writing the script until the last possible moment so that

frequently it was I who did it. The programmes were invariably pre-
ceded by a good lunch, usually in the flat, and on more than one
occasion he lost his place in the script and announced the records in
the wrong order. Sometimes he even fell into a doze while the
records were being played. But, thanks to John Lade, none of
these things was apparent to the listeners.

Autumn, a season I used to love before I worked for Gilbert,
unfailingly brought round the winter series of *Round Britain Quiz*.
It was the programme which I believed showed him at his best,
but I dreaded the recordings. Apart from the producer and the
studio staff, six people – Gilbert and Lionel Hale, two members of
the London team and two of the regional team – were involved,
all busy men, and to find a date and time when they could all be
available was a considerable headache. Unlike the producer's unhappy secretary, I had only one of them to cope with. But often five
or more dates would be discussed, fixed, and discarded again before anything was settled. That was no more than a minor problem
for me compared to the recording itself. For some reason, of which
no one seemed at all sure, this was one of the very few programmes
which was honoured with B B C 'hospitality' – which was translated
as a half-bottle of whisky for each of the two studios used. The members of the London team drank very little, so did regional members,
so, when they foregathered in one studio at the end of the recordings
Gilbert often tried to make up for the abstemiousness of his colleagues. In the last three years of his life I started the *Quiz* day in
the almost certain knowledge that my employer would come home
'tiddley', and my heart was in my boots from the moment I woke.
This behaviour was, of course, against his full will and desire.

He knew just how I felt, and before he left he would say: 'It's
all right, Podge. I promise you I won't have a drink after the
programme. I'll ring you the moment it's over and you can send
the car round to pick me up. *Stop worrying!*' And since no one
ever knew just when the recording might finish, this did nothing to
calm my nerves. It was sometimes two or three hours after the
recording was over that he telephoned, or arrived in a cab, to offer
long, improbable explanations of a member of the team arriving an
hour late, or the recording system breaking down, or – most
ingeniously unlikely of all – that it had been discovered at the end of
the session that the recording gear hadn't been working at all and
the whole thing had to be done over again. 'I only had time for a
very small, quick drink,' he would add, swaying and stumbling.

There were two personal television programme series which were a great success. In *I Know What I Like* Gilbert invited the viewers to share a variety of things he himself enjoyed – a painting, a sculpture, a song or orchestral recording, poems or prose he enjoyed reading, and sometimes an extract from a film or a play. In the other programme, a late-evening tele-recorded talk, for fifteen minutes he discussed anything that interested him, an item of news or a book or play, and sometimes he just grumbled about something or somebody. The press and public approved of them both. Of his late night talks, Maurice Wiggin wrote in the *Sunday Times*: 'They are always interesting, expansive and crackling with pungent good sense . . . He most enjoys talking about himself; and what a good talker he is when no one interrupts him. His unique act is to impersonate a schizophrenic who, so to speak, relaxes happily on the couch and treats the whole world as his psycho-analyst.' Another Sunday newspaper columnist described *I Know What I Like* as 'the best series television has given us this year'. But Gilbert himself finally began to call it 'I Like What I Know I Can Get', for so frequently half the items in his planned presentation had to be changed or abandoned because, in one way or another, they were unobtainable or impracticable.

In addition to these programmes, he was still appearing on *What's My Line?* and on a series of sound radio programmes called *On The Spot* in which, with the help of a team of reporters and commentators, he investigated matters of moment – smokeless zones, the eleven-plus examination, the motor-car industry, adoption, and the exchange of students between Britain and the United States. It was indirectly over this last programme that we had a most odd encounter with the press. After it had been broadcast, he invited an official of the American Embassy to his club for drinks. The following morning he told me, with amusement, how a discussion on differing education systems became so enthralling that Gilbert, waving his hands to emphasize a point, knocked a fellow-member's glasses off his nose and to the ground, where they shattered. That afternoon the reporter of a daily newspaper telephoned Gilbert; they had heard that he and his American guest had been involved in a violent argument which had ended with blows. Gilbert was furious and made that abundantly clear, at some length, to the reporter. Before he rang off, Gilbert heard the reporter remark, 'We didn't get much change there, let's try . . . (the American).' On this, Gilbert rang off and asked me to get his American friend on the telephone. I dialled the number and, as I did so, Gilbert picked up the extension on the table in the hall, where he was sitting. To our shocked amazement, we heard his own voice saying: 'And now, young man, I trust that you will go back to your News Editor and report to him that there is not a single word of truth in this preposterous and idiotic story. Tell him too – and you may use the strongest terms in your no doubt attenuated vocabulary – that if he prints a word of that lying rumour, I will sue the newspaper . . .' By some strange accident, the line of the newspaper office was still open and we were listening to a tape-recording of the conversation being played back!

That particular story was scotched. But around that time another – equally baseless – was maliciously offered for public gossip. Because a Wilfred Pickles programme was to be televised from Brighton within a few days of Gilbert Harding's *At Home* to Wynford Vaughan-Thomas, the Mayor of Brighton invited them both to a celebratory lunch. But Gilbert had planned a visit to his Aunt Edie in Hereford and would not be back in time, so, explaining why, he had to refuse. Other engagements, however, had to be fitted in and, eventually, the Hereford trip was postponed. Towards the end of the following week, a reporter telephoned to ask me what Mr. Harding had been doing in Hereford the previous Monday. He wasn't in Hereford, I told him; he was in Brighton, and I forgot the call at once. Two days later the newspaper's gossip columnist carried a paragraph suggesting Gilbert had turned down the Mayor's invitation because 'Harding and Wilfred Pickles aren't exactly buddies. Brighton's Publicity Manager said Gilbert was not at the luncheon because he was in Hereford. But Mr. Harding's secretary told me on the telephone that he was, in fact, in Brighton all that day.'

Two or three weeks before that time it had been announced by the B B C Press Office that the *At Home* television interview and the edition of *What's My Line?* a few evenings later would constitute Gilbert Harding's last appearance for some time, as he was once again going into hospital for a complete rest. It was said that he was suffering from a chest complaint. It was six months before he appeared again, and at least four months before the public were told that the 'chest complaint' was tuberculosis.

It had been discovered quite inadvertently when Gilbert visited his heart specialist for a routine check-up. The doctor said he was satisfied with the heart condition, but had detected some irregularity in the working of the lungs. He suggested an x-ray and this was taken one afternoon in Harley Street.

That evening Gilbert was taking me and a friend of mine to see Noël Coward's *Nude With Violin* and we had agreed that the three of us would meet in the theatre bar ten minutes before the curtain was to go up. As I was about to leave home for the theatre, Gilbert's doctor telephoned to me. He had been unable to get a reply from Weymouth Street and asked me to pass on a message to Gilbert that it was most urgent they should speak together that night. He then told me that the x-ray had revealed a small, but active tubercular patch on one lung and asked me if I felt able to break the news to him.

At the theatre I found Gilbert cheerful and high-spirited and was glad: he would be less likely to notice my own silences. He told me happily that the doctor who had taken the x-ray had said that the plates appeared to reveal nothing which might cause concern. 'You see, I said Dr. X was just an old alarmist fuss-pot. Let's drink to my wheezing pumps, as sound a pair of threadbare old bagpipes as you could wish to hear.' We found our seats and my companions both immensely enjoyed the performance. When it was over, as we stood in the entrance, Gilbert said: 'Now, where shall we go for supper. What about the Hungaria? It's only a step away . . .'

'Mr. Harding, please, before we talk about supper, your doctor is most anxious to talk to you and I think it would be better if you telephoned from your flat rather than a restaurant.'

'What nonsense! Doctors can wait until the morning. I'm hungry,' he protested.

But I insisted and, interpreting my looks, my friend took his leave. Gilbert, immensely puzzled, waited as I hailed a cab and not until he was seated in it did he say, 'Well, Roger?'

'I don't feel there is any need for alarm,' I said, as calmly as I could. 'The doctor wants you to talk to him because the x-ray plates have shown a small tubercular patch on one lung. He asked me to tell you.'

I was feeling deeply distressed and emotional myself, simply owing to the circumstances, and was prepared for equal distress and emotion from him. The reply, when it came, was utterly unexpected.

After a moment's silence, he said cheerfully: 'Thank Heaven for that! For years I have hoped for some malignant disease which

would end my life as quickly as possible with the minimum of discomfort. This, quite clearly, is it.'

I was astounded. Mainly by the extraordinary ignorance that
could believe tuberculosis to be any longer a mortal disease. But I
was also deeply moved because, having watched him more than
once physically and involuntarily fighting for breath and life when
his expressed wish was to die, I realized how he welcomed this
imaginary death sentence.

He telephoned to the doctor when we reached Weymouth Street
and reluctantly agreed to see a specialist in chest diseases. As he put
the receiver down, he turned to me and said gravely, 'I must see
him, I suppose. But, above all and beyond all, remember this, Roger.
I will not submit to being treated for this disease. No one shall make
me live against my will.'

He insisted once more when he saw the specialist next day. But
he, wisely and quietly, explained to Gilbert that his wishes in the
matter were of no account; doctor and patient must submit to the
law of the land. The specialist was by law obliged to report the case
to the local health authorities; the victim was equally obliged
to undergo the cure. Other people's lives must be protected. For
their sake he must prepare himself for six, perhaps many more
months in hospital.

CHAPTER ELEVEN

HOLIDAY MOOD

NEVER, I feel sure, has any patient been cured of T.B. with less discomfort to himself and more to his doctors, nurses and immediate circle of friends. University College Hospital can rarely have had a less co-operative patient; the staff can rarely have been subject to more exasperation. But, as always, of course, they finally achieved their object. And, as it turned out, more quickly than could have been hoped.

Deliberately, on the day he was due to enter the hospital, Gilbert got outrageously intoxicated. And within an hour of his being tucked up under the white coverlet, he was up, dressing, and insisting on returning to Weymouth Street. When we got him to bed again, he insisted that I leave his key-ring beside the bed 'in case I decide to return home during the night'. Finally, I left, feeling fairly secure in the knowledge that he was firmly asleep. I dragged myself home and into bed. I was still lying nervously awake when the telephone rang. Between starting from my bed and reaching the telephone in the sitting-room, the immediate future was vividly before me – the getting dressed, stumbling through the quiet, cold streets, soothing, pacifying, persuading and, finally, the conferring with doctors.

Apparently sober, deeply distressed, Gilbert at the other end of the telephone from his hospital bed said: 'Roger, I couldn't sleep without offering you my deepest apologies. I am utterly disgusted with myself and I want you to know it. I am upset beyond measure at the disgraceful way I have repaid all your kindness and trouble. Please believe me . . .'

Shivering with cold and with nervous tension, I was saying inside myself, 'Then, why, in heaven's name didn't you keep quiet and leave me to go to sleep?' but into the mouthpiece my voice was

F*

muttering, 'But of course I understand. I know exactly how you were feeling. Please don't worry about it for another moment. Just relax and go to sleep . . .'

From then on, his stay in hospital followed much the same pattern as before – the attempt to conform, the backslidings with cigarettes and alcohol, the stream of visitors. But constant care, rest and drugs – in spite of himself – did their work. After six weeks, the doctors said he could leave hospital, so long as he was prepared to stay indoors at Brighton until he was given permission to start work again. By the time Gilbert left his bed at U C H, I was more than ready to occupy it, so strenuous, for me, had been the cure. But the very fact that he was able for the first time to feel himself permanently at home in 20 Montpelier Villas, Brighton, gave Gilbert a new placidity. A Mrs. Hardy and her husband lived in the basement flat and she 'did' for Gilbert daily. Arthur Deeley and George, the former driver who had come to help out while Deeley's licence was suspended, mainly ran the household. Life went pleasantly and smoothly.

Although his doctors had set July as the earliest time when Gilbert could reasonably expect to be back at work, he was well enough to persuade them that he could take his usual place as chairman of *Twenty Questions* when it started again in the middle of May. A few weeks after that his diary contained almost as many engagements as it did before his illness. Unhappily, his first television appearance on his return was almost disastrous. He took part in a programme to mark the demolition of the old Gaiety Theatre in Aldwych. I could not see the programme myself, as I was on the way back to London from Yorkshire, but for many days afterwards people told me that he had seemed to have very little idea of what he was supposed to be doing. Some supposed that he had returned to work too soon; the less kindly suggested that he was drunk. But perhaps the saddest result was his estrangement from Nancy Spain.

She had, unwittingly, put herself in a position where she could not honestly refuse to criticize his performance in the *Daily Express*. She attacked his obvious lack of preparation and warned him that such a lackadaisical attitude might cost him his reputation. Gilbert, reacting instantly and emotionally, without taking the trouble or thought to ask her for an explanation, retaliated by sending Nancy a bouquet of thistles and writing a not entirely successful defence, under the headline, 'Oh, Nancy, you've hurt me', in his *People* column the following Sunday.

Soon his home life at Brighton was disrupted. First there was the discovery that he was suffering from a mild form of diabetes. His diet had to be readjusted and his consumption of pills increased; already he had to swallow about eight enormous tablets each day to control the tubercular tendency and now at least three more different tablets were added. Worse still was the departure of Arthur Deeley to get married and set up a home of his own soon after George, the temporary driver, himself not strong, had had to leave.

For the weekend of August Bank holiday that year, Gilbert invited Joan Smith to spend the holiday in Brighton. Because both George and Deeley had been given a holiday and he was without help of any kind in the house and so she had to do more cooking and housework than if she had stayed home in Bradford. Even more distressing was the fact that Gilbert had a minor heart spasm in the middle of the night and consequently had treated her to several displays of alarmed bad temper and irrational demands. Yet it was only a few days after she had returned to Bradford that he suggested, with enthusiastic delight, that she might perhaps be persuaded to come permanently to Brighton to run the household. By the end of the week, Joan had agreed. The basement flat was redecorated for her and about seven weeks later my new colleague, friend and ally assumed – unwittingly, I am afraid – a great part of the burden of trying to organize this unique personality.

Naturally, perhaps, the press seized on this as the possible basis for another 'romance'. Gilbert, Joan and I were constantly badgered for the inside story. It was almost impossible to pick up a newspaper without seeing a reference to 'Gilbert's Miss Smith'. It was a baptism of fire for Joan but her blunt, Yorkshire honesty carried her through it well – even on the occasion when, at a party, a rather intoxicated woman who had earlier been introduced to her with the now general phrase, suddenly exclaimed, 'Miss Smith, did you say? Gilbert's Miss Smith? I thought he said you were Gilbert's mistress!'

Within a few weeks of her arrival at Montpelier Villas, the household climate changed almost miraculously. Joan engaged a 'daily' to help with the housework. Mrs. Embery was her name, but to Joan and Gilbert and all their friends she was 'Midge' or even, formally, 'Mrs. Midge'. She is the original 'treasure' – efficient, hardworking, constantly cheerful, a counsellor and valued friend. Between them they managed to keep the Brighton house as calm, clean, tidy and orderly as any house which contained Gilbert Harding could ever hope to be. Joan's arrival gave Gilbert a new outlet,

too, for his delight in 'treats'. With her as his companion, he became
a regular theatregoer at Brighton, he enjoyed shopping expeditions
and visits to beauty spots and places of historic interest within a
comfortable run of his home. His social life widened, too, because
now that he had a hostess he was able to give more of the luncheon
and dinner parties that he enjoyed so much and, consequently, he
and Joan were invited to many more friendly functions in
Brighton.

To be offered a 'treat' by Gilbert was like being forced to pick,
blindfold, from a row of books on a shelf: with luck you might
choose enthralling, intellectual reminiscences, a collection of up-
roariously amusing anecdotes or even a cosy, high-class romance.
Or you might be unfortunate enough to put your hand on a nightmare story which would haunt you for weeks.

In the autumn of 1957 when we were once again busy with a
two weeks' session of *Housewives' Choice*, Gilbert stayed up in
London and gave me the most hectic fortnight I had ever experienced. Most of the day I was working at enormous pressure and
almost every evening he insisted on my accompanying him to some
theatre or restaurant. Those evenings were just like that shelf of
books and, naturally perhaps, the most vivid was the worst. We were
invited to the opening of a new restaurant just off Piccadilly and
by the time we arrived there, Gilbert was already quarrelsome. So
freely did he insult the guests that I only just succeeded in prevent-
ing one man from actually striking him. It was a great relief when
a fellow-guest, a close friend of Gilbert's, suggested that he should
carry him off to the Club and give me the opportunity to crawl
home. Between three and four o'clock the following morning, I was
awakened by the telephone. The same friend was calling to say
that he had taken Gilbert home to Weymouth Street, succeeded
in getting him out of the taxi and up in the lift but, once home,
Gilbert had collapsed on the hall floor outside his bedroom door
and refused to move. Now he was heavily asleep. Could I possibly
come over and help to get him to bed?

Though I knew from experience that it would take ten men or
a block and tackle to shift him an inch, I got dressed and made
my way through the shivery night to Weymouth Street. More worrying than the physical problems involved was the knowledge that
it could be disastrous if Gilbert should regain consciousness to
find me there. Only a few weeks earlier, in similar circumstances, I
had gone over in the dead of night to help get Gilbert to bed.

Unexpectedly, he had come suddenly to life and, lashing out all around him, had cursed me for being there. I was convinced that only my instant flight had saved me from considerable damage. So I explained to his friend that if Gilbert showed any signs of recovery, I must instantly disappear. We tried, but to no avail whatever, to lift him. The only thing to do was to make his cold and hard bed as comfortable as possible. I brought blankets to wrap round him and pillows to go under his head and, as I tucked in the last one, his eyelids flickered. Without hesitation, I slipped behind the nearest door, realizing even as I did so that, if Gilbert stayed where he was, my escape through the hall to the front door was completely blocked. I heard him struggle to his feet and there followed a bizarre and improbable game of hide-and-seek. On several occasions Gilbert wandered into the room where I was hiding, and it wasn't until his friend finally managed to persuade him into the kitchen to make coffee that I was able to creep out of the room, silently open the front door and scuttle down the stairs.

Yet, for an entirely different reason, I as vividly remember a train ride from Brighton in January 1958, only a few weeks later. I had gone down to Brighton early in the morning and since there was already snow on the ground, Gilbert decided that he would come up with me by train for his appearance in *Who Said That?* in the evening. The first sign of trouble came as Joan drove us to the station. The car skidded on a patch of ice, stalled and refused to start again. Fortunately, a taxi was passing, so we hailed it and reached the station with time to spare. Twenty minutes after the train was due to leave, it was still standing in the station. I had my head out of the window, looking for a porter to ask him to telephone Joan and get her to warn the producer, when the train started. It crawled for a few miles and stopped again. It moved on a little way and again halted. After this had happened four or five times, we agreed that there would be no time to call at Weymouth Street; Gilbert would have to go straight to the restaurant where the team were to meet for dinner. As the time arrived when the train should have reached Victoria, we seemed to be still only a few miles outside Brighton. Dinner, we decided, would have to be skipped and Gilbert would have to drive direct to the studio. In spite of the wintry weather outside, the compartment grew hotter and hotter. It seemed days since we had left Brighton. Finally it became quite clear that Gilbert would have to miss the programme altogether and, even worse, there was no way of letting the producer know the reason.

We eventually arrived at Victoria three and a half hours later and about twenty minutes after *Who Said That?* had ended.

The following morning's papers said 'Gilbert Harding in Great Rail Delay'; 'What Did Harding Say?' What Harding had in fact said, when it became abundantly clear that we were at the mercy of British weather and British Railways was, 'Roger, did you ever play the alphabet game?' We went solemnly through the alphabet, finding a county, a river, a town and a country beginning with each letter. We didn't have the faintest suggestion of a cross word until Gilbert firmly insisted that my contribution of the River Wandle, for 'W', did not exist and I was even more sceptical of his claiming a score with the River Wokooki, since he believed it to be in Australia, but declined to confirm through which state it flowed.

In May of that year, Gilbert decided that he would spend most of July holidaying in Denmark. We all looked forward to a holiday ourselves when, after a lot of discussion with the Danish Tourist Board, he announced that he would have the car shipped over there and be driven about by an experienced guide-chauffeur. I took my own break in June and almost looked forward to my return to work, with my boss away, when I would be able to settle each day's problems as they came along. It was a foolish hope. Within three days of his arrival in Denmark, I had had as many telephone calls from him asking me to attend to this, that and the other and adding a couple of dozen items to the list of jobs I had in the office. Then, perhaps shocked at the thought of his telephone bill, he took to writing and at least one letter and postcard arrived each day, exhorting me to further efforts. The last week of his stay arrived and I began to look forward to his return in good health and spirits.

Then, on the Tuesday night, came an urgent telephone call. I was to fly to Denmark by the earliest possible plane and let him know by telegram what time I was arriving at Aalborg airport, where he would meet me. He hinted at trouble and difficulties and finally instructed me to bring £100 in travellers' cheques.

It was already late at night. The Danish air line's London office was closed and the information desk at London airport assured me there was no connecting flight from Copenhagen to Aalborg, more than 200 miles to the north. In the early hours of the morning I was still poring over maps of Denmark. At midday on the following Friday Gilbert was due to catch the boat from Esbjerg to Harwich so, taking into account the many islands and stretches of water

I would have to cross between Copenhagen and Aalborg, it looked as though I was likely to arrive there just in time to make the journey to Esbjerg with him. I packed a bag in readiness and went to bed for the last few hours of the night, hoping that I would wake to find it all a dream. I didn't, but I did find in the morning that I could indeed fly from Copenhagen to Aalborg. I managed to get the last available reservation that day to Copenhagen, sent Gilbert a telegram to say I would be in Aalborg by 10 p.m. and set off.

I had a miserable journey. There were two hours to wait at Copenhagen airport and I thought it the most depressing one I had ever visited, in spite of the sight, as we circled it, of a dazzle of tiny coloured lights which I presumed to be the Tivoli Gardens. It was certainly a most casual journey: I caught my connecting flight to Aalborg only because I suddenly noticed that two nuns, who carried boarding cards of the same colour as mine, had passed through a glass door and were already crossing the tarmac to a waiting plane. They and I turned out to be the only passengers on a plane designed to carry sixty. The crew outnumbered us by two. I believed I had heard that nuns on an aeroplane are by some regarded as unlucky: almost I began to hope this might be true. But when, as we passed over the sea between Denmark and Sweden, I seemed to detect an irregular note in one of the engines, I looked under the seat to make sure my life-jacket was there.

My despair was miraculously lifted, however, by the enthusiastic welcome the apparently quite happy and only slightly intoxicated Gilbert gave me as I walked into the arrivals' lounge at Aalborg. He carried me off to the delightful remote country hotel where he was staying and I felt like a returned prodigal son as he guided me through a gargantuan dinner, urging on me delicacy after delicacy until I was completely incapable of another mouthful. With the coffee and brandy came the story of his 'difficulties' – and astonishingly slight they were, too. The trouble was that he found the company of his Danish chauffeur-guide exceedingly dull and there had been a few short but sharp exchanges when his companion hinted that his temporary employer was drinking too much. It was soon apparent that I had come to Denmark for three not very important purposes – to relieve Gilbert's boredom with his guide, to do his packing for the homeward journey and to keep him company on the voyage.

The following morning Gilbert was very cheerful. I began to

Ashford Castle

Telegrams
Telephone
CONG 3

CONG

CO. MAYO · IRELAND

Managing Proprietors:
NOEL HUGGARD
ANGELA HUGGARD

9.VII.59.

Dear Podge — Yr letter of 7th —

It was waiting here — many thanks —; and "here" is a lot of scenic — gastronomic — demi-paradise —

Please say "Yes" about the films — I have had an urgent letter from Wolf Mankowitz? for all that freely about transport : because I shall have John Duke — & I imagine that he will like

being about in studio.

But leave that be —

It's good news about Brian K — a very annoying about floods windows —

We sent him Pa & c — asking about replacing — I do hope that yr floor turn is better — try now —

Please sit — & write the Sisal Green — the carpet can wait. → for Dining Rm.

Yes — I meant the

A letter from Ireland. The question of the sisal carpet is still
unsettled.

feel that his holiday had done him a great deal of good. It was a cheerless day, but he decided that we would spend it driving around the North Jutland coast. As the day wore on, the greyness of the sea and sky began to have their effect: we stopped at one inn after another for 'something to cheer us up' until, by the time we returned to the hotel for dinner, Gilbert's face began to look as stormy as the sky. Shortly after we had finished dinner, both storms broke. A very drunken Gilbert turned on his guide, who had dined with us, and began loudly and elaborately to list his failings. The guide, who bore an ancient and once much-honoured Danish title, retained his dignity and his temper – but only just. He rose and left us. 'I will not be driven another kilometre by that dreary, stuck-up Great Dane,' Gilbert shouted after him. But the charming and patient hotel manager and I, between us, convinced him that it was too late to find a new driver that night and that we could leave it until morning. We were both, of course, assuming that a night's sleep would change his mind. As the evening grew late, I tried to persuade Gilbert that it would be better for him to go to bed, in view of the early start next day, but finally I abandoned the effort and it was almost five o'clock when he fell asleep in his chair and I slipped upstairs to start the packing. Half an hour later I came down again, deciding to try shock tactics. Briskly, I shook his shoulder and dragged at his arm – 'It's time for bed, Mr. Harding,' I ordered. Docilely he rose to his feet, followed me up the stairs and was in bed and asleep again within five minutes.

Two hours later, when I was called, I went to waken him. He was already awake, very lively and quite recovered again. After breakfast, when he asked me to pay the hotel bill, I realized why I had been asked to bring the travellers' cheques: I needed all the £100 and more for his week's stay there with the guide. We left much later than we had planned, but thanks to the extremely skilful work of the driver – after some persuasion, still the same one – we arrived at Esbjerg with half an hour to spare. After three nights with very little sleep, I prayed that Gilbert would go to his cabin reasonably early that night. But my prayers went unanswered. Not only did he head straight for the bar and stay there, but this turned out to be the roughest North Sea crossing the crew had experienced that summer. About twenty people, including Gilbert and me, felt able to face dinner, but by nine o'clock the ship was deserted save for six or seven of us in the bar. Finally we were alone except for the tired, bored barman. What seemed like hours later, when I had

listened over and over again to the story of his Danish tribulations,
I suggested I might see him to his cabin and then retire myself.
'Why?' he demanded. 'Because I'm tired,' I said despairingly. 'Well,
hump you,' said Gilbert. 'You're paid to look after me, not to complain that you're tired.' For the first and only time, I made no
attempt to restrain my impulses to hit him. With the flat of my
hand I gave him a blow across the shoulders. Gilbert slithered off
his stool to the floor. He looked up at me in amazement. 'What
happened?' he asked. 'The ship rolled and you fell off the stool.
You really would be better off in bed.' 'You're absolutely right, my
boy,' he said. 'Help me up.' I gave him my arm and we left the bar
in complete amity.

After we docked at Harwich, I drove with Gilbert to a village near
Colchester where he was to stay the night before opening a village
fête the following day, left him settled there, caught a train to
London, was in bed by ten and slept until the middle of Sunday
afternoon.

It was Joan who had the mixed pleasure of sharing Gilbert's last
holiday. In 1959 he decided to spend three weeks touring in Ireland,
finishing with several days in Dublin. He particularly wanted an
open car, so he traded-in the little Hillman, which was always kept
at Brighton, for a Morris 1000. It was to be shipped across from
Fishguard and Joan was to drive him from Cork to Kerry, to
Limerick, up to Connemara and then across to Dublin. The hotels
had been booked in advance, the glorious summer showed every sign
of continuing and Gilbert was longing to taste good Irish bacon
again. He and Joan set off for Fishguard on a wave of optimism.
For Gilbert it was justified. In Ireland – save for the presence of
other English tourists – he felt entirely at home. Talking and drinking were his favourite occupations: here he was surrounded by like-
minded companions whenever he wished. But poor Joan had not
only to endure the apparently interminable evenings and persuade
him finally to bed, but she had to be awake and alert enough to
drive him the following day on the next stage of his journey. For the
last holiday of Gilbert's life, it was a splendid and momentous one –
it all but gave Joan a nervous breakdown.

CHAPTER TWELVE

'AND PEACE AT THE LAST'

THE last words of Gilbert Harding's autobiography, *Along My Line*, were, 'I do wish that the future were over.'

It was at about half-past five in the afternoon of November the sixteenth 1960 that for him the future was over. The man who had been so afraid of the agony of dying, though he longed for death, fell dead on the steps of the B B C studios in Portland Place, after a recording of his favourite programme. Except that the manner of his death alarmed and upset those around him, it was how he would have chosen to die.

It happened only about two months after a television programme that had made a nation-wide sensation – his *Face to Face* interview with John Freeman. This had revealed a Harding largely unknown to the television public; it headlined one or two sides of this many-sided man that had previously been known only to his household and his friends.

Some time before, soon after the early successes of *Face to Face*, it had been reported in the press that Mr. Freeman had said, 'I hope that Gilbert Harding will be one of my subjects,' and, 'I am going to do Gilbert Harding.' Realizing the enormous possible interest of such an encounter, the press seemed to conspire to make it a certainty. But to all inquiries Gilbert said that he had not heard any such proposal. And when the B B C producer asked him to agree he instinctively, if not very firmly refused.

He knew well by now the 'Gilbert Harding image' that existed in the mind of his public. In his various aspects he was what the man in the street would have liked to have been – a champion of justice, one who did not suffer fools gladly, one who always spoke his own mind, a man who could afford to live well but who had care and compassion for those who could not, a rebel against authority. All these clichés came to life in the minds of his readers and viewers. And they were all, to a greater or lesser extent, true. Moreover, they were all generally admired characteristics among the British.

But these were the scales of the public armour he wore. He was frightened that he might be turned over on his back, like a turtle, to expose his vulnerability to pity or mockery. He often sought private sympathy for physical or mental suffering because he wanted to be assured of personal concern; public concern embarrassed him. It was the same fear that led him to conquer his physical weakness for the length of any public appearance and which made him, for as long as he could, write of his illness as 'shortage of breath', when he knew that it was heart disease.

Not that, I think, he ever knew quite how bad it was. During that same year, he had to fly to Edinburgh for a recording of *Round Britain Quiz*. The confinement of an aeroplane, the waiting on the tarmac, the queueing at the steps were irritants to be avoided. But B E A, with fine impartiality, were unable to co-operate without some official cause for doing so. Could I produce a medical certificate? They sent me the requisite form, which I, in turn, sent to the doctor in Brighton. He posted it back to me in London and I forwarded it to B E A. But not before I had taken note of the reason it gave for special treatment – 'Emphysema . . . toxic myocarditis'. The next day, when Gilbert arrived in London, he asked me if the journey was arranged. I said it was.

'And have you organized it so that I can manage it without choking to death? What about that doctor's certificate?'

'That's been done,' I said. 'I got it from Brighton and sent it straight to B E A.'

'What ever did you do that for? I wanted to see what it said. Didn't you look at it? What *did* it say?'

I tried to remember. 'Emphy—' I started.

'Emphysema,' he caught up impatiently. 'Well, of course – just that the lungs have lost their elasticity so that one can't breathe. Naturally. That is clearly apparent.'

But later, surreptitiously, I looked up all the words in a medical dictionary. What was in fact clearly apparent was that they implied a fatal condition. I think if he had known this he would have ceased to demand special treatment. An embarrassing public spectacle of weakness would have nauseated him: death would be a release.

Yet fear itself was frightening. When the B B C finally pressed him to take part in *Face to Face*, Gilbert agreed. It was the courage of a shy man that drove him to bravado. And the producer, in sympathy, gave him an escape clause. The interview would be filmed and if, when it was over, Gilbert still wanted to veto it, he could, so that it need never be broadcast.

The question Gilbert dreaded – the question that was bound to be asked – was, 'Why have you never married?' Here was the really vulnerable spot. I feel certain that had he married early an intelligent, readily emotional woman like his mother, Gilbert would have been a very different man. He needed the security of unquestioning affection to bolster his innate shyness. But I have always supposed that, so deep was his natural timidity, the first refusal he had had was sufficient to confirm his feeling of inadequacy. Later it was his physical condition that defrauded him of sexual consolation.

But when, in fact, the *Face to Face* interview was televised, it unexpectedly placed the public firmly on Gilbert's side. It is an English convention that a man on the defensive is a man to be supported. On this occasion, it seemed to me, the viewers just could not understand what John Freeman was getting at. Everyone I talked to afterwards, even people who knew him well, said: 'But why did Freeman keep on and on about punishment and pain and discipline? It had no relation to Gilbert at all!' I understand that Mr. Freeman was advised by a psychiatrist on the questions he should ask in *Face to Face* and it may well be that to the expert this programme was a fascinating study. To the simple viewer it represented a cruel probing into an honest, emotional, unhappy man. And they rose to his defence. They were unutterably shocked that John Freeman had not, it seemed, taken the trouble to find out that Mrs. Harding had died – as had her daughter and Gilbert's only sister – painfully of cancer. Thousands among the public knew, because they had read every word printed about their own special 'telephoney'. When Freeman said, 'Have you ever watched anyone die?' the desperately controlled tears, the choked voice as Gilbert managed to nod a faint 'Yes', might have been their own.

When the Monday morning papers arrived, with their comments on the programme, Gilbert was astonished. He was even more amazed when each mail brought hundreds of letters of sympathy. The press and the public had been suddenly shaken by this new Harding. 'A deeply unhappy man . . .'; 'the death-wish . . .'; 'the face without a future . . .'; 'Where did he choose the wrong line? . . .' The open hostility to John Freeman shocked him; it was, he felt, entirely unjustified. At the first possible opportunity he telephoned to Mr. Freeman and told him so, without reservation. In his *People* column the following Sunday he took the first public opportunity to say quite plainly that John Freeman had been doing just what was expected of him and that it was unfair and unjust to criticize him.

Nevertheless, it was that programme which prepared the public for Gilbert's death. I, of course, had been prepared for it very much longer – mentally and emotionally, from the time when I had been warned by the doctor nearly two years earlier; practically, during his grave illness in University College Hospital in March, 1959. We had then all feared that he was on his death-bed. The priest had seen him, the doctors appeared defeated. His solicitor said, sensibly and unemotionally, 'Roger, if Gilbert does die, we must all be ready for it. We all know what he wants. If we make our plans now it will be easier to carry them out when the time comes.' So, in a lucid moment, we decided all the details and formalities, which were not, as it turned out, required until more than a year later.

At the time it had really seemed that there was no hope. Gilbert had been taken ill in Edinburgh, where he had gone for a *Round Britain Quiz* recording, but, fortified with drugs, had managed, with my anxious help, to get back to London. Deeply disturbed, I had already telephoned from Scotland to his doctor, who was waiting for us when we reached the flat. The doctor, equally disturbed, was determined that Gilbert should at once enter a nursing home, and by telephone found a bed in one a few hundred yards from the flat. As usual, he was installed only under violent protest and urgent persuasion, and this time one night was sufficient, as he thought, to cure him. When the doctor arrived for his morning visit, such was the fury of Gilbert's mood that for forty-eight hours he fought to return home. Then, on the promise that day and night nurses would be engaged, he was allowed to do so. But only twenty-four hours later came an evening of queer unreality. The doctor called and the specialist followed. He called a consultant, who in turn called another. Gilbert sat on a hard, straight chair in his bedroom, breathing all the time through his oxygen mask, seeming to take little notice of the experts who came to consider his condition. Joan and I and Susie, the pug, slid quietly in and out as we were needed.

It had much earlier been arranged that at six-thirty Kate Wad-leigh should come on from the office to get his column for next Sunday's issue of *The People* and, though we had warned her of Gilbert's condition, he had refused to allow her to be put off. She came into the 'office' to be faced with a hushed and frightened atmosphere. The four doctors were conferring in the sitting-room; Gilbert was in the next room, barely breathing. Kate held on to Susie and we continued to wait. There was a sound from the bed-room and Joan went in. 'He wants to see you, Kate,' she said. And when Kate had taken the briefest moment to assure him that his column could wait until the next day or the day after, she hurried back, overcome by his weakness. But it was a physical weakness only, for a few moments later, when Joan peeped in at him again, he whispered through his oxygen mask, 'Kate hasn't gone, has she? Take in the bottle of Scotch and give her a drink. She must be tired out!' There had been hundreds of times when we three had commiserated with each other about the minor ailments which Gilbert magnified with moans and groans and four-syllable medical descriptions (his bruises were always 'contusions'). It was suddenly and vividly apparent that when he had reached a situation where he had ceased to care about the sympathy of others he still cared about their comfort.

The result of the doctors' conference was severe and conclusive. Gilbert must go immediately into hospital under the strictest pos-sible conditions. A bed was booked at University College Hospital and, even had he wanted to, Gilbert was given no chance at all to protest. It was apparent to us all that his life was seriously in danger. Once he was installed in the hospital bed, despite his hatred of confinement, he had to submit to an oxygen tent. Throughout the week that followed Joan or I, or both of us, were by his bedside or near at hand in the hospital until finally, despite Gilbert's will, despite the doctor's despair, he began suddenly to take hold of life again. Within a shorter time than any medical authority might have predicted he was back on his feet again and insisting on his release from hospital.

At such a time it became lastingly clear that this man, of whom some have since said and written, 'He had hundreds of acquain-tances, but no friends,' was held in very deep affection. Perhaps those who, apart from his family, would feel personally bereaved by his death numbered no more than about a dozen. But these, both men and women, had known him at his worst, had endured every aggressive defence he might adopt, and still remained aware of the man beneath the armour. And, beyond that small circle, were the hundreds to whom he had given comfort, help and hope – unwittingly, perhaps – through his identification with the cause of that mythical creature (whose identity he never accepted) 'the man in the street'.

A great proportion of those who looked on him in this way were poor people – widows, parents of a large family, old people. Because of his own upbringing, as the child of a working widow, he knew what poverty meant. He never ceased to remember and the memory coloured all his life, because he was never free of the fear that he might end his life in poverty. It made him worry endlessly about the cost of doctors and drugs, even while they gave him relief from pain; it incited him often to endless small, complicated 'fiddles' that would save a few shillings. It led him, too, into wild generosities when he thought of others in the same plight.

Many of those who wrote to him were sick or crippled. As a boy his health had been 'frail'; as a man he suffered constantly. So again he could understand. In the Union Workhouse, at Hereford, he had been brought up in an atmosphere where there was strict justice, constantly tempered with mercy. He hated injustice and he despised and detested unjust, merciless officials.

Though frequently intolerant himself, he constantly fought for tolerance. He had a favourite phrase about not disliking someone because 'his skin is a different colour, his nose of a different shape, or his creed of a different melody'. The colour bar was abhorrent to him. One day he had invited a West Indian legal friend to lunch when, at about midday, a very old friend of his, a South African barrister, telephoned him and suggested a meeting. 'Come at once,' said Gilbert with great delight. 'I've got a most interesting lawyer arriving any minute for lunch and we'll find another chop for you. It will be splendid!' The West Indian arrived and, half an hour later, the barrister. Gilbert rose to greet him and made the introductions. The barrister bowed coldly, said, 'Just a moment, Gilbert,' and turned back into the hall. Gilbert followed him, puzzled. 'Really, Gilbert!' he protested. 'What ever has come over you? I couldn't possibly sit down to lunch at the same table with that man.' It was only at that moment that Gilbert realized what had gone wrong. 'Well, I really *am* sorry,' he said, with a charming smile. 'That means I can never again sit at a table with you! . . . Roger! I am afraid Mr. X is leaving and will not be visiting us again. Please shut the door very firmly behind him.'

I am certain that when he went back into the sitting-room he had ready on his tongue an explanation for his friend's departure that must have immediately quietened any faint stirring of embarrassment. Gilbert, when he was himself, had an instinctive awareness of the feelings of others.

It may have been noticed in this book that I never addressed my employer throughout the seven and a half years I worked for him, other than as 'Mr. Harding'. And for all that time I was constantly and permanently grateful that he never once questioned that rigid formality. It was my badge of office. In his world of radio, television and newspapers everybody seemed to call everybody by his Christian name within minutes of meeting. Gilbert called me 'Roger' on the day I started work with him, but if he had insisted on my calling him 'Gilbert', I should have quit the job. Even when he was savagely drunk and my nerves were strained to screaming point, I still hissed at him '*Mr. Harding, be quiet!*' It was the fine, taut barrier between us and a familiarity that might have bred worse than contempt in such a situation.

I found it fascinating, after his death, to study the characteristics attributed to him by those whose words were published the following day. All of them seemed to emphasize his nobility of character, his loneliness, his unhappiness. No one mentioned his humour. You would have thought he never had a gay moment in his life. Yet surely almost anyone who knew him at all well must have spent at least one riotous half-hour in his company. All the time I knew him, he could, when he was well and sober, keep a handful of people breathlessly delighted with his stories and fighting to restrain their laughter lest they should miss one word of his narrative. The quoted appraisal of Kenneth Adam, Controller of Television Programmes, ended with the words 'incapable of malice'. But he *boasted* of his malice! Often, when I arrived in the morning, Gilbert was bursting to tell me the story of some really wounding remark he had made the previous night to puncture the pomposity of an acquaintance. He might, if he cared enough about the man's feelings, telephone him later to apologize, but as long as the malicious triumph lasted he would retail it with glee. Like every other part of the entertainment business, radio and television bristles with gossip, intrigue and backbiting. Though it bored Gilbert to be personally drawn into

these squabbles – unless they deeply involved him – he could build
up each absurd little incident into an enthralling ten-minute saga
which would reduce his audience to helpless laughter.

About 1955, I think, *The People* commissioned Roger Wood to
take a series of photographs of Gilbert for use with his column in
that newspaper. The sitting produced about twenty-five proofs,
every one of them typical of some accepted Harding mood. They
were given to Kate for her appraisal and she brought them for me
to look at. When we had sorted them through, she said: 'That's
one I'm going to get enlarged for myself.' It was the same one I
had instinctively chosen. Roger Wood had caught a 'benevolent'
expression – the twinkle in the eyes, the cheeks rounded in a smile,
the moustache bristling with good humour – Gilbert at his unbeat-
able best. But to anyone who knew him well there was instantly
apparent behind the twinkle, behind the humorously curved
mouth, the sly thought: 'I can stay like this for just thirty seconds
more. Then I shall start quoting chunks of the Holy Bible, fly into
a fury or tell you the funniest story you've heard in the last twelve
months!' It was, I suppose, the reason why – though I must have
been sacked half a dozen times and resigned as often – I knew I
could never willingly give up the job and accept life with a lesser
man. Gilbert Harding's secretary might find his work exhausting to
the point of extinction, his health, nerves and temper frayed to
tatters, but it was a life full of an infinite richness of experience.

When I watched the Memorial programme televised on the BBC
on the Sunday night after his death, I began to feel 'This is pitched
too high. Why must they all lay the emphasis on his intellectual
qualities, not on his humanity?' It was when Jean Metcalfe described his sudden appearance to join them unexpectedly, at a
family lunch in the kitchen, that I got back to normal. The occasion
was very vivid in my mind. I was the reason for that unexpected
visit. Gilbert had been invited to the christening of Jean's youngest
baby, which was to be on a Wednesday, so when he telephoned me
from Brighton the preceding Wednesday, saying, 'What time is
Jean's baby's christening, and where have I to be?' I looked in
the diary and told him, never dreaming that he thought that this
was the very day. Off he went to Jean's house for, as he thought,
the christening, only to find the family tucking into boiled bacon
in the kitchen. He must have been immensely puzzled. And so, even
though he had greatly enjoyed the visit, he took it out of me. For
days afterwards he would introduce me to everyone – friends and

strangers alike – with 'Have you met Roger Storey, my brilliant secretary? Not only does he not know what day of the week it is, he doesn't know what week of the year it is, either!'

After Gilbert's death, Bernard Braden, for whose home and family Gilbert had a great affection, said of him, 'The real tragedy about Gilbert was that his special talent was impromptu conversation – and that has gone out of date.'

I am sure Mr. Braden was wrong – not about Gilbert's talent, but in his suggestion that there was no place for it. Many people have called Gilbert 'the Dr. Johnson of our times' and, from such of Boswell as I have read, I can believe this to be true – so far as comment and conversation were concerned. Unhappily, unlike Dr. Johnson, Gilbert Harding was no writer. True, he often referred to himself, with pride, as 'a journalist', but he convinced himself, bitterly, more than once, that he was no writer. 'Something goes wrong between my brain and the pen: the words I am saying in my head are pungent and rounded; by the time they have flowed through my hand and my pen they are flat, dull and pompous.' That was why his weekly columns, his occasional articles and his books, were all dictated. There was no barrier between his mind and his *tongue*.

The ordinary man becomes aware, long after the moment has passed, of the brilliant riposte he might have made, the devastating argument he should have offered, the illuminating comment he alone could have contributed. With Gilbert there was no such lapse. He responded instantly. The riposte, the argument, the comment were immediately ready on his lips because, behind the blanket of lethargy and self-pity in which, towards the end, he wrapped himself, his mind was always briskly and eagerly alive.

In the BBC's Memorial television programme, Sir Compton Mackenzie said: 'Never again shall we sit, on opposite sides of the fireside, talking into the small hours.' The last time that Gilbert visited Edinburgh and sat on the other side of the fire from Compton Mackenzie, I had the unforgettable privilege of being there too. It was one of the great occasions of my life. Just as, sandwiched between the daily routine of telephone calls and letters and appointments, there were the visits of people like John Betjeman or Sir Hugh Foot – great figures of our day on whom I had the good fortune to eavesdrop.

And yet, when Dame Edith Sitwell was approached by the BBC to do a broadcast interview and agreed to their suggestion that the interviewer should be Gilbert Harding, I had to soothe and comfort him into a sufficient degree of self-confidence to accept. He was as full of timidity and self-denigration as a schoolboy presenting himself for examination. Later we learned that Dame Edith had been just as nervous as he.

When, in the turmoil of practical detail that followed his death, we came to choose a prayer to be printed on the official card for the Solemn Requiem Mass at Westminster Cathedral on the ninth of December 1960, I gratefully recognized this prayer of Cardinal Newman:

'May He support us all the day long till the shades lengthen, and the evening comes, and the busy world is hushed, and the fever of life is over, and our work is done.

Then in His mercy may He give us a safe lodging and a holy rest, and peace at the last.'

They were words he had often read to me and I know they were a lasting comfort to him. I pray they have come true.